DON WEEKES

PUCK-STOPPIN' TRIVIA

GREYSTONE BOOKS

Douglas & McIntyre Publishing Group

Vancouver/Toronto/New York

For Gerry Halton, for saving the day in so many ways, so often.

— Don Weekes

Greystone Books
A division of Douglas & McIntyre Ltd.
2323 Quebec Street, Suite 201
Vancouver, British Columbia   V5T 4S7

Canadian Cataloguing in Publication Data
Weekes, Don.
  Puck-stoppin' trivia
  ISBN 1-55054-710-0
  1. Hockey goalkeepers—Miscellanea. 2. National Hockey League—Miscellanea. 3. Hockey—Miscellanea. I. Title.
GV848.76.W44 1999   796.962′27′0922   C99-910474-8

Editing by Anne Rose and Kerry Banks
Design by Peter Cocking
Typesetting by Brenda and Neil West, BN Typographics West
Cover photo by John Giamundo
Printed and bound in Canada by Best Book Manufacturers
Printed on acid-free paper ∞

The publisher gratefully acknowledges the assistance of the Canada Council for the Arts and of the British Columbia Ministry of Tourism, Small Business and Culture. The publisher also acknowledges the financial support of the Government of Canada through the Book Publishing Industry Development Program for its publishing activities.
Canada

Don Weekes is a television producer and writer with CFCF 12 in Montreal. This is his twelfth hockey trivia quiz book.

CONTENTS

PREFACE

After dropping three straight games to Washington during the 1998 Eastern Conference finals, Dominik Hasek appeared at morning practice before Game 5 sporting "Kramer, Swiss Cheese" across the shoulders of his jersey. Nicknamed "Kramer" by his teammates (after the off-centre *Seinfeld* character), Hasek, in the spirit of levity, was poking fun at himself for playing like Swiss cheese. He had blown Game 4 by allowing two stunning Capital goals—the second a 60-foot sleeper from Joe Juneau. The loss was only a hiccup in Hasek's career season, which included an Olympic gold medal and a second MVP title, but it came in hockey's most important season—the playoffs.

And what of Hasek's playful yet self-deprecating crack, comparing his netminding to a cheese full of holes? The truth was that Hasek's demanding season had simply worn him down. Living with the demands of being the most dominant player on his team, mental fatigue set in after 72 regular-season games, six Olympic matches and 13 playoff games—91 gruelling contests in total. Unfortunately for the Sabres, the fade came in Games 2 and 3, with overtime losses against Washington. Hasek's lapses led to frustration: in Game 2 he threw his blocker at Peter Bondra; later, in Game 4, he inexplicably tackled Richard Zednik. The Dominator's infallibility wavered, and the middle-of-the-pack Sabres were badly shaken after Juneau's goal wiggled past Hasek's catching glove. As hockey writer Michael Ulmer reported, Hasek's "presence radiated through the Sabres' lineup. He emboldened forwards, kept an unspectacular corps of defensemen afloat and made Buffalo impervious to the demoralizing effect of bad goals."

The job of goaltending has always attracted unique personalities. Braving repeated assaults of vulcanized rubber launched at 90 miles per hour, goalies are the team flakes: eccentric loners and outcasts who, in hockey's early days, worked on their mechanics and psyches in isolation and played their game ill-equipped and under-coached, always facing the spectre of serious injury, employment uncertainty and public scrutiny. Yet no one player can singlehandedly effect the outcome of a game more than the goalie. Who wouldn't develop some eccentricities under such pressure?

The evolution of the goalie's status has come slowly, along with better scouting, space-age gear and coaches who specialize in developing mental and physical agility. But as goalie John Davidson has said, "The shots got harder before the equipment got better."

Even after more than a century of pain and punishment, of endeavour and invention, guarding the net still demands the same essential qualities. Goalies will always be the last line of defense in the world's fastest team sport.

In this twelfth book in our series on hockey trivia, we step between the pipes and visit the job site of Dominik Hasek, Ed Belfour and Patrick Roy. We look back at the careers of the game's greatest netminders, testing your hockey smarts on a range of events and personalities, from one-game wonders to Stanley Cup champions. Watch your five-hole!

DON WEEKES
JANUARY 1999

Visit my Web site at: **www3.sympatico.ca/don.weekes/**

1

HEAD GAMES

The greatest strength of a goalie may be in his head. No matter how good his physical skills are, if a goalie can't maintain a strong mental game after a bad goal or period, a goalie won't make it in the big leagues. In our opening chapter we fire off a battery of general questions from every position on the ice to test your trivia agility. Stay sharp and don't self-destruct. After all, a bad goal, like a wrong answer, doesn't mean the game is lost.

(Answers are on page 6)

1.1 Who is known as Mr. Goalie?
A. Montreal's Ken Dryden
B. Chicago's Glenn Hall
C. Detroit's Terry Sawchuk
D. Buffalo's Dominik Hasek

1.2 What is the highest number of shots Patrick Roy has faced in a regular-season NHL game?
A. 40 to 45 shots
B. 45 to 50 shots
C. 50 to 55 shots
D. More than 55 shots

1.3 After Patrick Roy, which starting goalie played the highest percentage of his team's games during the 1990s?
A. Ed Belfour
B. Kirk McLean
C. Patrick Roy
D. Bill Ranford

1.4   Which NHL team drafted Dominik Hasek and, later, traded him to Buffalo?
A. The Hartford Whalers
B. The Minnesota North Stars
C. The Chicago Blackhawks
D. The Philadelphia Flyers

1.5   What unusual event *almost* ended Arturs Irbe's career after his spectacular 1993-94 season with San Jose?
A. He sustained injuries mountain climbing
B. He was bitten by his dog
C. He suffered a concussion in a roller hockey match
D. He was diagnosed with a rare disease

1.6   Which celebrated NHL goalie made a surprise visit to the USSR dressing room just before Game 1 of the 1972 Canada-Russia Summit Series?
A. Jacques Plante
B. Glenn Hall
C. Ken Dryden
D. Tony Esposito

1.7   Who is Fast Eddie?
A. Ed Mio
B. Ed Belfour
C. Ed Giacomin
D. Gary Edwards

1.8   How much money was Boston Bruins minor pro goalie Jim "Ace" Carey guaranteed to make with the AHL's Providence Bruins in two seasons, 1998-99 and 1999-2000?
A. $250,000
B. $500,000
C. $1 million
D. $5 million

1.9 Which goalie won the Calder Trophy as rookie of the year over Steve Yzerman in 1984?
A. Tom Barrasso
B. John Vanbiesbrouck
C. Pelle Lindbergh
D. Ed Belfour

1.10 What is the highest number of Olympic Gold medals won by a goalie?
A. One medal
B. Two medals
C. Three medals
D. Four medals

1.11 Which netminder played tandem with four future Hall of Famers?
A. Ed Chadwick
B. Al Rollins
C. Denis Dejordy
D. Cesare Maniago

1.12 As of 1998, how many goalies have won the Hobey Baker Award, given to the best player in U.S. collegiate hockey?
A. None
B. Only one
C. Three goalies
D. Five goalies

1.13 How much does it cost to "rent" a goalie to play in recreational hockey leagues in Canada?
A. About $30 per game
B. About $50 per game
C. About $75 per game
D. About $100 per game

1.14 What incident suddenly ended the stellar NHL career of Bernie Parent in 1979?
   A. An on-ice injury
   B. An acrimonious trade
   C. An unfair benching
   D. A player contract dispute

1.15 Despite being best friends, which two opposing goalies duked it out in a 1998 brawl that saw all 12 players on the ice ejected from the game?
   A. Detroit's Chris Osgood and Colorado's Patrick Roy
   B. Washington's Olaf Kolzig and Boston's Byron Dafoe
   C. Dallas' Ed Belfour and Philadelphia's Ron Hextall
   D. Tampa Bay's Daren Puppa and Pittsburgh's Tom Barrasso

1.16 Among WHA goalies who later backstopped in the NHL, who was the last to retire?
   A. John Garrett
   B. Richard Brodeur
   C. Pat Riggin
   D. Mike Liut

1.17 Among Vezina Trophy-winning goalies, who played the fewest games in his career?
   A. Detroit's Johnny Mowers
   B. Buffalo's Bob Sauve
   C. Philadelphia's Pelle Lindbergh
   D. Montreal's Richard Sevigny

1.18 As of 1998-99, how many goalies have scored a goal in the NHL?
   A. Three goalies
   B. Five goalies
   C. Seven goalies
   D. Nine goalies

1.19 Where is the five-hole?
A. Low to the goaltender's stick-side
B. Between the post and the goaltender's catching glove
C. Between the goaltender's legs
D. It's the distance between the shooter and the goaltender

1.20 Who was the youngest goalie to register 400 wins?
A. Terry Sawchuk
B. Tony Esposito
C. Patrick Roy
D. Grant Fuhr

1.21 Which goalie of the 1990s had the best career goals-against average?
A. Dominik Hasek
B. Martin Brodeur
C. Patrick Roy
D. Ed Belfour

1.22 How small was the shortest goalie to see NHL action?
A. Five foot one
B. Five foot three
C. Five foot five
D. Five foot seven

1.23 Who is the NHL's biggest goalie?
A. Olaf Kolzig
B. Ron Hextall
C. Sean Burke
D. Tom Barrasso

1.24 Which goalie is best known for playing a key role in starting a fight that led to a team brawl before the start of a 1987 playoff game?
A. Philadelphia's Chico Resch
B. The Islanders' Billy Smith
C. Edmonton's Grant Fuhr
D. Philadelphia's Ron Hextall

1.25 Since the NHL Amateur or Entry Draft began in 1969, what is the highest draft position awarded to a goalie?
A. First pick overall
B. Second pick overall
C. Third pick overall
D. Fourth pick overall

1.26 Currently, about 260 players are drafted each summer at the NHL Entry Draft. What is the highest number of goalies ever selected in one draft year?
A. Between 20 and 30 goalies
B. Between 30 and 40 goalies
C. Between 40 and 50 goalies
D. More than 50 goalies

1.27 Among those goaltenders who spent their entire career with one team, who played the most games?
A. Chicago's Charlie Gardiner
B. Toronto's Turk Broda
C. Montreal's Ken Dryden
D. Chicago's Tony Esposito

HEAD GAMES
Answers

1.1 **B. Chicago's Glenn Hall**
No puckstopper in NHL history deserves the moniker Mr. Goalie more than Glenn Hall; few have had such an impact on their profession. In fact, today's netminders all have a little of Hall in their style. Hall revolutionized the position with his butterfly stance, and honed the fundamentals of skating, puck-handling and positioning as one of the elite goalies of the 1950s and 1960s. In 1990s parlance, he "got game."

1.2 **C. 50 to 55 shots**
On December 10, 1997, Roy, a 12-year veteran, faced a career-high 53 shots and allowed two goals in a 2-2 tie with the

Toronto Maple Leafs, of all teams. Colorado was outshot 53-19 in what Avalanche coach Marc Crawford called, "our worst (performance) of the season." Worse still, Roy sustained strained abdominal muscles after making the 51 saves and was sidelined for four games.

1.3   D. Bill Ranford

While most of the league's busiest goalies played on average about 61 per cent of their team's games, Roy and Ranford stayed healthy and had the confidence of their clubs to backstop approximately 10 per cent more games during the 1990s. Of a possible 784 games between 1989-90 and 1998-99, Roy stepped between the pipes an amazing 75 per cent of the time; Ranford 70 per cent.

The NHL's Busiest Goalies in the 1990s* (by percentage)			
Goalie	**Teams**	**GP**	**PCT**
Patrick Roy	Mtl/Col	591	75%
Bill Ranford	Edm/Bos/Wsh/TB/Det	551	70%
Ed Belfour	Chi/SJ/Dal	527	67%
Curtis Joseph	St.L/Edm/Tor	524	67%
John Vanbiesbrouck	NYR/Fla/Phi	510	65%
Mike Richter	NYR	492	63%
Kirk McLean	Van/Car/Fla	478	61%
Andy Moog	Edm/Bos/Dal/Mtl	431	61%
Felix Potvin	Tor/NYI	380	61%
Current to 1998			

1.4   C. The Chicago Blackhawks

Hasek's career moves off-ice are as unique as his acrobatic goal-tending style. In fact, a number of teams failed to recognize his full potential while he was within their reach. Hasek was drafted an incredible 199th by Chicago in the 1983 draft—late in the 11th round. The Hawks obviously weren't gambling much on the unknown 18-year-old, whose immediate plans lay in playing for his hometown team in Pardubice, Czechoslovakia. When he finally hit the NHL in 1990-91 and 1991-92, Hasek notched a 2.53 goals-against average in 25 games. But Hawks general manager Mike Keenan preferred the red-hot Ed Belfour; he sent Hasek to Buffalo. A year later at the 1993 NHL Expansion Draft, the Sabres, unimpressed after a mediocre season, left Hasek unprotected when the newly formed Anaheim Mighty Ducks and the Florida Panthers were filling their ranks. However, neither expansion team picked Hasek. He stayed in Buffalo to become the class of the NHL, winning multiple Vezina Trophies, First All-Star Team appearances and the coveted MVP award twice (a league first for goalies). Ironically, Hasek's first NHL victory came against Buffalo in a 5-3 Chicago win March 8, 1991.

1.5   B. He was bitten by his dog
The Sharks' impressive 58-point turnaround in 1993-94 and a seven-game, first-round playoff victory over the heavily favoured Red Wings amounted to what was supposed to be Arturs Irbe's coming-out year as a top-flight NHL goalie. He was brilliant in goal and a bonafide sports celebrity in San Jose and the Bay area. But that summer, Irbe suffered severe damage to both hands after being mauled by his dog in his hometown of Riga, Latvia. While working out, Irbe knocked the sleeping hound by accident. The dog woke and went wild, biting his startled owner's hands. After it was over, Irbe had cut tendons and nerve damage. "I was really worried. It was serious damage. I thought I might not play again," he later said. The dog had to be put to sleep.

1.6   A. Jacques Plante
Before the opening game of the 1972 Summit Series, Vladislav Tretiak received an unusual visit from NHL veteran Jacques Plante, who, through a translator and with blackboard diagrams, instructed the young Soviet goalie on how to stop Canada's top snipers (including Phil Esposito, Pete Mahovlich and Yvan Cournoyer). Whatever possessed Plante, perhaps hockey's most learned goalie, to reveal such hockey secrets is not clear; perhaps he felt sorry for Tretiak, a fellow gatekeeper up against overwhelming odds. But the game is now hockey

lore. The Soviets humiliated Canada 7-3, exposing Canada's biggest weakness—its lack of game preparation, particularly in properly assessing Soviet strengths, such as Tretiak. After the loss, Mahovlich unwittingly remarked that Tretiak had played him like he'd known Mahovlich throughout his career, which leads us to wonder how Plante reacted to Canada's defeat that night. Was he smiling at his tutorial success, or regretful?

1.7   C. Ed Giacomin

During New York's 53-year drought between Stanley Cups, the Rangers had a few inspirational puckstoppers who nearly altered the fortunes of the Cup-starved club. Both Chuck Rayner (1950) and John Davidson (1979) reached the finals in their eras, but neither garnered the kind of intense loyalty that Ranger fans lavished on Giacomin. Fast Eddie played 10 seasons in New York, led the league in victories three times and helped the team reach postseason on nine occasions. His peak came in 1972 when the Rangers lost a tough six-game final series against Bobby Orr and the Boston Bruins. In late October 1975, New Yorkers were stunned to learn that Giacomin, 36 years old, had been sent to Detroit. On his first return to the Big Apple later that year, Madison Square Garden erupted in a deafening ovation to salute their faithful goalie. Today, Fast Eddie is the only Rangers goalie in history whose sweater number has been retired by the club.

1.8   D. $5 million

Instead of basking in the NHL spotlight in 1998-99, Carey, once Washington's Vezina-winning superstar goalie, was riding buses in the AHL, all the while collecting a $5-million salary. After his Vezina year in 1996, Carey slumped so badly his free fall from greatness landed him with the Bruins' AHL farm team in Providence. With a guaranteed salary of $2.3 million on a one-way contract, Boston management was obligated to pay him $5 million for 1998-99 and 1999-2000. Carey lobbied for a buyout in the summer of 1998, but the Bruins resisted. In late 1998-99 the club sent him to St. Louis, where he played just four games. Carey is the highest-paid player in American League history.

1.9   A. Tom Barrasso
In 1983-84, 18-year-old Steve Yzerman stepped into the NHL straight from junior hockey and had a rookie season most NHLers only dream about—scoring 39 goals and 48 assists to lead Detroit with 87 points. But Yzerman, chosen fourth overall in the 1983 draft, couldn't outscore the fifth pick, Barrasso, in Calder balloting. Barrasso, 18, also cracked the big leagues without playing one game on the farm, by compiling a strong 26-12-3 rookie record and the league's second-best average, 2.84. Besides winning top rookie honours, the Sabres freshman nabbed the Vezina Trophy and berths on both the NHL First All-Star Team and the NHL All-Rookie Team. Other rookie goalies who beat rookie snipers include: Ed Belfour over Sergei Fedorov (1991) and Ken Dryden over Rick Martin (1972).

1.10   C. Three medals
Vladislav Tretiak, the goaltender with the most wins in international competition, played in 19 Olympic games between 1972 and 1984, won a record three gold medals (in 1972, 1976 and 1984) and one silver (in 1980) with a red-hot goals-against average of 1.74. In World Championship competition, Tretiak backstopped a record 10 world champions. In 98 games he produced a goals-against average of 1.92.

1.11   D. Cesare Maniago
Maniago's early career in hockey is a classic example of the frustrations faced by goaltenders trying to break into the NHL during the six-team era. Between 1960-61 and 1966-67, Maniago was shuffled around to nine minor-league teams while waiting for his NHL opportunity. During his seven-year wait he started just 55 NHL games while backing up Hall of Famers Johnny Bower in Toronto, Jacques Plante in Montreal and Ed Giacomin in New York. Maniago's big break came when Minnesota selected him in the 1967 Expansion Draft. He backstopped the Stars for nine seasons, five of those in tandem with his fourth Hall of Famer, Gump Worsley. (By no means is Maniago an exception. At least three other goalies—Terry Sawchuk, Bruce Gamble and Don Simmons—played with four Hall of Famers.)

1.12 B. Only one
The only goalie to capture the Hobey Baker Award is Robb Stauber, the Los Angeles Kings' fifth-round choice (107th overall) in the 1986 Entry Draft. Stauber capped his outstanding sophomore season at the University of Minnesota by being named the top U.S. college player in 1988, after leading the Gophers to the regular-season championship and establishing Minnesota records in wins (34), games (44) and shutouts (5).

1.13 A. About $30 per game
Anyone who has played recreational hockey knows of the empty-net syndrome. When the regular goalie doesn't show up for a game, teams are forced to shoot at the post or a jersey hanging from the crossbar. For a fee of $25 or $30 per game, teams can hire within an hour of game time mercenary goaltenders from rental services. Some goalies in the netminder-for-hire business play as many as three games per day, pocketing about $18 of the $30 fee.

1.14 A. An on-ice injury
On February 17, 1979, Philadelphia's Bernie Parent suffered a fluke eye injury when a stickblade pierced the unprotected eye space of his goalie mask in a game against the New York Rangers at the Spectrum. The injury—two small tears in the conjunctiva of his right eye—ended Parent's stellar career, which included two Vezina Trophies as top goalie, two Conn Smythes as playoff MVP and two Stanley Cups, all during the Flyers' heyday of the mid-1970s.

1.15 B. Washington's Olaf Kolzig and Boston's Byron Dafoe
Sitting pretty with three first-period goals, Bruins coach Pat Burns sensed the fight coming. "You could feel it when we got the big lead in the first period. It's something that goes back to last year's playoffs," Burns said. At the 12-minute mark, Burns's "feeling" turned ugly, erupting into a 12-player free-for-all that pinned best friends Kolzig and Dafoe in a toe-to-toe dance amidst the debris of hockey equipment, blood and bodies strewn over the ice. Referee Mark Faucette tossed all 12 players

and assessed 264 minutes in penalties in that first period. "It's tough fighting your best friend. You can joke about it all you want, but when you're out there it's tough to throw a punch," Kolzig said. Boston prevailed over Washington 5-4 in the game, November 22, 1998.

1.16 D. Mike Liut

Liut, St. Louis' fifth choice in the NHL's 1976 draft, signed with Cincinnati in 1977 and played the last two seasons of the WHA. After the WHA folded in 1979 Liut was reclaimed by St. Louis, and in 1981 he was named to the NHL's First All-Star Team. Liut also played for Hartford and Washington before retiring in 1992 after 663 NHL games and a 294-271-74 record. He is the last WHA goalie to play in the NHL. Garrett hung up his pads in 1985; Brodeur and Riggin stuck around until 1988.

1.17 A. Detroit's Johnny Mowers

Mowers took over from Normie Smith in the Red Wings cage in 1940-41, just after World War II broke out. But Mowers was no wartime substitute, rightfully winning the starting job and eventually the Vezina in 1942-43 with a 25-14-11 record and a league-leading six shutouts, more than the combined total of shutouts by all goalies in the rest of the NHL. In 1943, Mowers also joined the war effort, as a member of the Canadian air force. But unlike other NHL starters who went off to war, such as Turk Broda, Frank Brimsek, Sugar Jim Henry and Chuck Rayner, when Mowers returned he found his old job filled by a quality replacement, Harry Lumley. With Lumley in the Detroit net, Mowers played only seven games in 1946-47. His miserable 0-6-1 record and recurring back problems ended his career, and the former Vezina winner retired after only 152 games. Pelle Lindbergh, Philadelphia's Vezina winner in 1985, recorded the next-fewest games, playing in just 157 games (only five more than Mowers) before he died in an auto accident, just months after winning the top goalie honour.

1.18 B. Five goalies

As of 1998-99, only five netminders—Billy Smith, Ron Hextall, Chris Osgood, Martin Brodeur and Damian Rhodes—have potted goals in league history. The Islanders' Billy Smith got credit for scoring on November 28, 1979, but he did not shoot the puck himself. Hextall, Osgood, Brodeur and Rhodes all fired the puck through traffic into their opponents' empty net (vacated for the extra attacker). Hextall did it twice with the Flyers: on December 8, 1987, and later in playoff action, on April 11, 1989. Osgood, with the Red Wings, scored his empty netter on March 6, 1996; Brodeur got his on April 17, 1997, the league's second postseason goal by a backstopper; and Rhodes received credit for a first-period goal on January 2, 1999.

1.19 C. Between the goaltender's legs

The five-hole is one of the five holes in a goalie's coverage of the net: the upper and lower corners on both sides of the netminder, and the space between his legs. When modern goalies quit stacking their pads and adopted the butterfly stance (to move faster laterally from post to post and to stop low shots more effectively) it gave shooters this fifth hole in which to score. With their legs split apart at the knees in the inverted-V position, goalies opened themselves up to more shots than ever before. However, despite the butterfly's flaws, its advantages outweigh the risks (at least for some netminders). Because the play of today's game is so fast, shooters can afford little time to get a shot off. As a result, most shots come along the ice. Goalies such as Patrick Roy use the butterfly to drop to their knees more quickly, to tighten the five-hole and create a wall of pads across the ice. As former netminder Chico Resch explains in Bruce Dowbiggin's *Of Ice and Men*: "They say Patrick Roy goes down in the butterfly all the time and it's true. He's giving you a few inches at the top of the net and he's saying you can beat me up there, but under pressure that's a tough shot."

1.20 C. Patrick Roy

As of 1998-99 only six goalies have broken the 400-win mark. Each had the good fortune of playing on winning franchises and staying healthy. Perhaps the most fortunate is Roy, who began his NHL career at age 20 in 1985-86. Except for a couple of hiccups Roy has never waned in the win department; he bagged his 400th victory in his 14th season on February 5, 1999. (The historic win came in a 3-1 victory over the Detroit Red Wings, the team Terry Sawchuk, the next-youngest 400-win goalie, played with for much of his career.) Roy was just 33. Sawchuk became the NHL's first 400-victory goalie in 1965 at age 35. Other members of the 400 Club are Grant Fuhr (at age 36), Glenn Hall and Tony Esposito (at age 40) and Jacques Plante, the oldest goalie to hit 400 wins, at age 42.

1.21 B. Martin Brodeur

After his first six complete seasons of 2.40, 2.45, 2.34, 1.88, 1.89 and 2.29 with the defensive-minded New Jersey Devils, Brodeur's career goals-against average of 2.19 represents the best mark among goalies in the 1990s. But he is sixth on the list of all-time career averages. The best career average in NHL hockey is 1.91, shared by old-time netminders Alex Connell and George Hainsworth, both of whom had started their careers before forward passing rules were modified, in 1928-29 (see Chapter 4).

1.22 B. Five foot three

Roy "Shrimp" Worters, a 12-year NHL veteran with the New York Americans and the Pittsburgh Pirates, stood only five foot three and weighed just 135 pounds. Yet despite his tiny size, Worters played much bigger, winning the Vezina Trophy as top goalie in 1931 and playing five complete seasons without missing a game. His diminutive appearance also clashed with his fiery temperament, which made him a fierce competitor both on-ice and off. Worters's contract demands with the Pirates in 1928 forced his trade to the New York Americans. When Worters refused to report, NHL President Frank Calder suspended the star netminder. He was only reinstated at a special Board of Governors meeting in December 1928. His outstanding play in goal that season kept the Americans on top and earned Worters the first Hart Trophy awarded to a goalie. Only four other netminders since Worters have received such a tribute. Worters never won the Stanley Cup, but he was named to the Hall of Fame in 1969. (Another small goalie was John Roach, who weighed only 130 pounds and was five foot five.)

1.23 C. Sean Burke

Although hockey's position players have grown bigger in the last 30 years, goalies have too. There are fewer Gump Worsleys (five foot seven, 180 pounds) in the league today and more Kolzigs (six foot three, 225 pounds). Kolzig, who stands equal to Hextall and Barrasso, is among the NHL's tallest goaltenders. But Sean Burke (and Daren Puppa at six foot four, 205 pounds) leads all cage men, measuring six foot four, 208 pounds, a full four inches taller than many of the biggest old-timers, such as Terry Sawchuk, Glenn Hall and Frank Brimsek, who were all six foot. But that four-inch difference among this select group of goalies is slightly misleading. If you take 21 of today's top netminders (from John Vanbiesbrouck at five foot eight to Burke at six foot four) they average about six foot—three inches taller than a comparable group of old-time goalies.

1.24 A. Philadelphia's Chico Resch

During the 1987 Wales Conference finals between Montreal and Philadelphia, a bizarre pre-game brawl erupted after the warmup in Game 6. Chico Resch and Ed Hospodar tried to prevent two Canadiens players from performing their pre-game ritual of shooting the puck into the Flyers' empty net. (In previous games, Claude Lemieux and Shayne Corson would stay on the ice to pot a goal after both teams had left the ice for their dressing rooms.) The Flyers didn't like the routine, so mild-mannered Resch and hitman Hospodar were elected as on-ice watchmen. Resch picks up the story in Dick Irvin's *In the Crease*: "I threw my stick to try and knock the puck away from him (Lemieux). I was still in the mood that this was just fooling around. Hospodar took a different approach and he charged at Lemieux and jumped him.... I skated over and yelled at him, 'Ed, what are you doing?' And Lemieux looked up and he says, 'Yeah Ed, what are you doing?' Within seconds both teams had poured out onto the ice, some players half-dressed and with bare feet. A full-scale brawl ensued for 11 minutes before officials were notified and able to restore order. The league handed out $24,000 in fines.

1.25 D. Fourth pick overall
Until the 1998 Entry Draft no goalie had ever been drafted higher than Ray Martiniuk (1970—Montreal), John Davidson (1973—St. Louis) and Tom Barrasso (1983—Buffalo), who each went fifth in their respective drafts. Then, the New York Islanders, with an eye on history and the fourth and fifth overall choices in 1998, picked Val D'or goalie Roberto Luongo fourth (and blueliner Eric Brewer fifth), making him the highest goalie ever selected. Other top picks include Michel Larocque (sixth—1972—Montreal), Jamie Storr (seventh—1994—Los Angeles), Grant Fuhr (eighth—1981—Edmonton) and Jimmy Waite (eighth—1987—Chicago). (Prior to 1969, when team sponsorships still played a role in the availability of juniors, the highest-drafted goalie was Michel Plasse, who was chosen first overall by Montreal in 1968.)

1.26 B. Between 30 and 40 goalies
About 20 of the world's best young goalies are drafted each year by NHL teams, but in 1993 that number almost doubled. Typically, most of these 36 players went low in the draft. The top netminder selected was the Quebec junior player-of-the-year Jocelyn Thibault, who the Nordiques chose 10th overall. Thibault is only the sixth goalie to appear in the NHL as an 18-year-old. Other notables from the 1993 draft include Tommy Salo, picked 118th by the New York Islanders, and Patrick Lalime, taken 156th by Pittsburgh. In 1996-97 Lalime broke Ken Dryden's record for the longest undefeated streak by a rookie with 14 wins and two ties.

1.27 B. Toronto's Turk Broda

Although other veteran netminders have played hundreds more games, among those who have worn just one team sweater throughout their careers, Broda is in front by a wide margin. The Maple Leaf backstopper played in 629 regular-season games and 101 postseason matches in 14 seasons from 1936-37 to 1951-52, interrupted only by two years of military service during World War II. Closing in on Broda's mark is Mike Richter with 492 games, as of 1998-99. Dryden quit Montreal after 397 games; Brodeur, so far, has logged 375 games with New Jersey; Esposito played 873 games in Chicago, but his first 13 matches were as a Montreal Canadian.

Longest Careers of One-Team Goalies*

Goalie	Team	Years	GP
Turk Broda	Toronto	1936 to 1957	629
Mike Richter	NYR	1988 to present	492
Ken Dryden	Montreal	1970 to 1979	397
Bill Durnan	Montreal	1943 to 1950	383
Martin Brodeur	New Jersey	1991 to present	375
Chuck Gardiner	Chicago	1927 to 1934	316
Greg Stefan	Detroit	1981 to 1989	299

Current to 1998-99

GAME 1

BEEZER AND THE EAGLE

It has often been said that hockey's best nicknames have gone the way of the barefaced goalie and the 50-game schedule. While it is true that in "the good old days" nicknames were so common that they virtually replaced players' given names in the stats columns (Gump Worsley, Red Kelly), does any fan today not know who the Dominator is? According to our roster below, the best aliases might be playing right now. Match the 23 goalies from the 1980s and 1990s on the left with their nicknames on the right.

(Solutions are on page 118)

1. _____	Curtis Joseph	A.	The Dominator
2. _____	Felix Potvin	B.	Godzilla, or Olie the Goalie
3. _____	Mike Vernon	C.	Tomcat
4. _____	John Vanbiesbrouck	D.	St. Patrick
5. _____	Ed Belfour	E.	The Wizard of Oz
6. _____	Tom Barrasso	F.	The Mask
7. _____	Mike Richter	G.	Kidder
8. _____	Ron Hextall	H.	CuJo
9. _____	Martin Brodeur	I.	The Cat
10. _____	Dominik Hasek	J.	Coco
11. _____	Andre Racicot	K.	Red Light
12. _____	Grant Fuhr	L.	The Eagle
13. _____	Jim Carey	M.	Brody, or the Door
14. _____	Andy Moog	N.	Captain Kirk
15. _____	Bill Ranford	O.	Mooger
16. _____	Kirk McLean	P.	Hexy
17. _____	Olaf Kolzig	Q.	T-Bo
18. _____	Jocelyn Thibault	R.	Super Salo
19. _____	Trevor Kidd	S.	Beezer
20. _____	Arturs Urbe	T.	Archie
21. _____	Chris Osgood	U.	Vernie
22. _____	Tommy Salo	V.	Ricky Rod
23. _____	Patrick Roy	W.	Billy the Kid

2

GOALIE FIRSTS

In more than 80 years of hockey there have been about 70 father-son combinations in NHL history. Many pairings have been skaters; the most famous present-day dad-son combo being Bobby and Brett Hull. Other bloodlines have given hockey a few skater-goalie tandems, such as Bryan Jr. and Ron Hextall. But only a few NHL netminders have produced goaltending sons of NHL-calibre quality. Who was the first father-son goalie pair? In this chapter we look at some of the more unusual goalie "firsts" in NHL history.

(Answers are on page 23)

2.1 Who was the first NHL goalie to be named league MVP since expansion in 1967?
A. Pete Peeters
B. Patrick Roy
C. Grant Fuhr
D. Dominik Hasek

2.2 Who was the first American-born goalie to record 300 NHL wins?
A. John Vanbiesbrouck
B. Frank Brimsek
C. Tom Barrasso
D. Mike Richter

2.3 Which old-time goalie was the first netminder pulled to add an extra attacker?
A. Georges Vezina in the 1920s
B. Tiny Thompson in the 1930s
C. Turk Broda in the 1940s
D. Gump Worsley in the 1950s

2.4 Although NHL teams didn't use tandem goalies until the 1950s, in which year were two goalies first named to a Stanley Cup champion?
A. 1928-29
B. 1938-39
C. 1948-49
D. 1958-59

2.5 Which Detroit netminder was the first NHL goalie to face two penalty shots in one game?
A. Roger Crozier
B. Gilles Gilbert
C. Glen Hanlon
D. Mike Vernon

2.6 In what schedule did an NHL goalie first record 40 or more wins?
A. A 50-game schedule
B. A 60-game schedule
C. A 70-game schedule
D. An 80-game schedule

2.7 A shot from which NHL scoring star finally drove Jacques Plante to don hockey's first regularly worn goalie mask?
A. Detroit's Ted Lindsay
B. Montreal's Maurice Richard
C. Chicago's Bobby Hull
D. New York's Andy Bathgate

2.8 What famous hockey first was little-known New York Rangers backup Joe Schaefer involved in?
A. The NHL's first masked goalie, Jacques Plante
B. The NHL's first goal by a goalie, accredited to Billy Smith
C. The NHL's first female goalie, Manon Rheaume
D. The NHL's first scoreless tie, by Clint Benedict and Jake Forbes

2.9 Considering the NHL began operations in 1917-18, in which decade did the first father-son goalie combination record shutouts?
A. The 1930s
B. The 1950s
C. The 1970s
D. The 1990s

2.10 Who is the first NHL netminder to win an Olympic goal medal in a shootout?
A. The U.S.A.'s Jim Craig
B. Canada's Trevor Kidd
C. Sweden's Tommy Salo
D. The Czech Republic's Dominik Hasek

2.11 Who was the first goalie scored upon by his brother in NHL action?
A. Tiny Thompson in the 1930s
B. Tony Esposito in the 1960s
C. Gary Smith in the 1970s
D. It has never happened

2.12 Which goalie from the 1970s was the first netminder to jump directly from junior into the NHL?
A. Ken Dryden
B. John Davidson
C. Billy Smith
D. Gilles Gilbert

2.13 In what decade was a goalie first scored upon in a penalty-shot situation in a playoff game? Name the goalie.
A. The 1920s
B. The 1940s
C. The 1960s
D. The 1980s

2.14 Which old-time goalie faced the NHL's first penalty shot ever awarded in a Stanley Cup final?
A. Montreal's Bill Durnan
B. Chicago's Mike Karakas
C. Detroit's Harry Lumley
D. New York's Davie Kerr

2.15 After the NHL was formed in 1917-18, how long did it take before a goalie received credit for an assist?
A. 19 seconds
B. 19 minutes
C. 19 games
D. 19 seasons

2.16 Who was the first European goalie to win the Vezina Trophy as top NHL netminder?
A. Valdislav Tretiak
B. Pelle Lindbergh
C. Dominik Hasek
D. Arturs Irbe

2.17 In what decade did two goalies fight for the first time in NHL playoff action?
A. The 1920s
B. The 1930s
C. The 1940s
D. The 1950s

2.18 Who was the first NHL goalie on record to face more than 2,000 shots in a season?
A. St. Louis' Mike Liut
B. Hartford's Greg Millen
C. Edmonton's Grant Fuhr
D. Philadelphia's Pelle Lindbergh

2.19 Who was the first goalie to record three consecutive 2,000-shot seasons?
A. Grant Fuhr
B. Curtis Joseph
C. Felix Potvin
D. Dominik Hasek

2.20 Which 400-game goalie was the first NHL netminder to play for three different teams in one season?
A. Greg Millen
B. Kirk McLean
C. Sean Burke
D. Jim Rutherford

GOALIE FIRSTS
Answers

2.1 D. Dominik Hasek
The Hart Trophy, awarded to the player most valuable to his team, has seldom gone to goaltenders. In fact, when Hasek won the Hart in 1997, he became the first goalie so honoured in 35 years, the longest drought between goalie winners in league history. During 1996-97 Hasek compiled the league's best-save percentage (.930) and a 2.27 goals-against average to carry the struggling Buffalo Sabres to their first divisional championship in 16 years. When Hasek won the venerated trophy again in 1997-98, he became the first goalie ever awarded consecutive Harts and the first back-to-back winner since Wayne Gretzky, who won the trophy in 1986 and 1987.

2.2 C. Tom Barrasso
Heading into the 1997-98 season, Boston-born Tom Barrasso (295 wins) and John Vanbiesbrouck (288 wins), of Detroit, Michigan, were each poised to break the 300-win plateau. On October 19, 1997, Barrasso beat Florida 4-1 to become the first U.S.-born goalie with 300 victories. Coincidentally, Barrasso's 300th win came by outduelling his rival, Vanbiesbrouck, who

collected his number 300 just months later on December 27, 1997, in a 6-2 win over the Islanders.

2.3   B. Tiny Thompson in the 1930s
The first goalie yanked for an extra attacker was Boston's Tiny Thompson, who got pulled in the dying moments of a 1-0 game in the 1931 Boston-Montreal semifinals. The strategy to replace Thompson with an extra forward, in an attempt to score the tying goal, was the inspiration of Bruins coach Art Ross. Although Boston still lost to Montreal 1-0, the day's sports pages called it an "amazing manoeuvre," and it soon caught on, becoming a standard game plan in hockey everywhere.

2.4   A. 1928-29
The first time two goalies from the same team were co-credited on the Stanley Cup was in 1928-29, when Boston won the championship backstopped by famed goalkeeper Tiny Thompson. Thompson played the entire 44-game schedule and every game of the playoffs, but he shared the championship with goalie Hal Winkler, who is listed as Boston's "sub-goaltender" on the Cup. Considering it was in the era before two dressed-to-play netminders, what happened? Apparently, though Winkler didn't start a single game in 1928-29, his name was etched on the Cup (and his picture included in the official team photo) for sentimental reasons after he performed admirably in the 1927-28 finals against Ottawa. Boston lost that 1928 Cup, and, when Winkler was replaced by Thompson the following year, many on the team felt that he deserved to be part of hockey's greatest award.

2.5   B. Gilles Gilbert
On February 11, 1982, referee Kerry Fraser established an NHL first when he awarded Vancouver's Thomas Gradin and Ivan Hlinka penalty shots in the third period against the Wings' Gilles Gilbert. Both Canuck players scored on Gilbert in the 4-4 tie, establishing two firsts: two penalty-shot goals in a single game and in a single period.

2.6   C. A 70-game schedule
During the 50- and 60-game schedules of the 1940s, goalies and their teams usually averaged in the 30-win range. That changed in 1950-51 with the 70-game schedule and Detroit's Terry Sawchuk, a rookie who played all 70 contests that year and won a record 44 games. Sawchuk became the first netminder in NHL history to break the 40-win barrier (as the Red Wings became the first team to break 40). Amazingly, he repeated the feat the following year—another 44 wins in 70 games. To put Sawchuk's accomplishment in perspective, no modern-day rookie has ever equalled his 44-win record, even in today's 82-game schedule.

2.7   D. New York's Andy Bathgate
Before Plante revolutionized hockey by wearing hockey's "first" mask on November 1, 1959, goalies routinely had their faces carved up by pucks and sticks and required hundreds of stitches. (Before donning his mask, Plante himself had 200 stitches, four broken noses, a fractured jaw and cheekbones and a hairline fracture.) Facial injuries were considered an occupational hazard, and masks the devices that impaired eyesight and implied weakness. But the shot that ended Plante's barefaced days was a Bathgate backhand that, according to the Rangers forward, was a "get-even" shot aimed deliberately at the Canadiens goalie's face. Plante had levelled Bathgate earlier in the game, sending him crashing into the boards. Bathgate retaliated with a short backhand that struck Plante on the right cheekbone and nose, cutting him badly. Plante left the ice bloodied, received the necessary stitchwork and returned with his crude face guard in place and a new resolve never to go maskless again.

2.8   A. The NHL's first masked goalie, Jacques Plante
One of hockey's least-known details about that fateful night in 1959, when Jacques Plante first wore his famous mask, concerns the Rangers' statistician and seldom-used spare, Joe Schaefer. Plante's Montreal Canadiens were playing in New York when, as Ranger netminder Emile "the Cat" Francis tells

the story, "After Andy Bathgate's backhand forced Plante into the Garden's medic room for stitching, Jacques gave coach Toe Blake two options: 'Play me with my mask or get yourself a backup.' In those days the home team supplied both teams with the spare goalie, and in New York, it was Joe Schaefer. Earlier, Joe had played for Chicago and he let in nine goals in 18 minutes. After the game the press boys say, 'Was it a thrill to play tonight?' And Joe says, 'Oh yeah.' They ask, 'What's your weakness?' Joe says, 'Shots!!!' Well, Blake knew Schaefer's reputation for soft goals. So when Plante refused to play without his mask Blake's choice was obvious. Plante wore his mask. When he skated out, I couldn't believe it."

2.9 C. The 1970s

Among the 70 fathers who passed on their hockey genes to produce NHL-playing sons, only two dad-son combinations have been goalie combos. The first was Sam and Pete LoPresti, who became the NHL's first father-and-son tandem to record shutouts February 8, 1975, when Pete zeroed Philadelphia in a 5-0 Minnesota win. Father Sam recorded four shutouts for Chicago in the early 1940s. Both are American-born goalies. The second father-son pair is Dennis and Pat Riggin. Each recorded at least one shutout, with son Pat's first coming in 1979-80.

2.10 C. Sweden's Tommy Salo

The first gold-medal game decided by a shootout was at the 1994 Olympics, when Peter Forsberg scored on the 13th shootout penalty shot and Paul Kariya missed on the 14th, giving Sweden their first-ever gold medal in Olympic hockey. Corey Hirsch was Canada's scapegoat, while Tommy Salo (of the New York Islanders) became a national hero in Sweden.

2.11 A. Tiny Thompson in the 1930s

Only a few brothers have become NHL skater-goalie combinations. Before Phil and Tony Esposito became household names in the 1970s, Brian and Gary Smith played against each other in 1967-68, when Brian was with Los Angeles and Gary in Oakland. But the first brothers combo to face each other were

Paul and Tiny Thompson. In what is considered the first occurrence of one brother shooting and scoring on another brother, Paul, a forward with the Chicago Blackhawks, scored a goal against Tiny, a Boston Bruins netminder, in a 2-1 Hawks loss on December 21, 1937.

2.12 B. John Davidson
It's not that unusual today for goalies to jump from junior to the ranks of the NHL, but when St. Louis drafted Davidson fifth overall in 1973, he went directly from the Calgary Centennials in the Western Canadian Junior Hockey League to the Blues, playing 39 games in 1973-74. Davidson was 20 years old.

2.13 C. The 1960s
After only two penalty shots were awarded (and both stopped) in 50 years of postseason play, Terry Sawchuk of Los Angeles gave up the first penalty-shot goal on April 9, 1968. Sawchuk was beaten by Minnesota's Wayne Connelly as the Stars beat the Kings 7-5.

2.14 A. Montreal's Bill Durnan
The first penalty shot ever awarded in a Stanley Cup final came on April 13, 1944, when Bill Durnan stonewalled Chicago's Virgil Johnson, one of the few American-born players in the NHL at the time. The call was made by referee King Clancy. The Canadiens won the game 5-4 and the Stanley Cup in a four-game sweep over Chicago. It was Montreal's first championship in 13 years.

2.15 D. 19 seasons
The first NHL goalie to receive credit for an assist was Boston's Tiny Thompson; he earned the famous point in a 4-1 Bruins win over Toronto on January 14, 1936. Goalies had certainly earned assists prior to Thompson, but because assists often went unrecorded during the NHL's formative years, there are few statistics detailing those offensive gains. We do know that Montreal's Georges Vezina earned an assist without credit on December 28, 1918, after teammate Newsy Lalonde picked up

a rebound from a Vezina save, skated the length of the ice and scored in a 6-3 win over Toronto.

2.16 B. Pelle Lindbergh

In his fourth NHL season, 1984-85, Swedish sensation Pelle Lindbergh blossomed into the league's top goalie, leading Philadelphia with a personal record of 40-17-7 to best the Edmonton Oilers in regular-season standings 113 to 109 points. Lindbergh also led the Flyers to the Stanley Cup finals. The Oilers won the Cup but Lindbergh's mobility and lightning-quick reflexes proved his worth as he outballoted Buffalo's Tom Barrasso for the Vezina that year. Only months later, Lindbergh died in a high-speed, alcohol-related car crash. He was 26.

2.17 C. The 1940s

Probably the earliest fight between two netminders in playoff action came on April 10, 1948, when Toronto's Turk Broda and Harry Lumley of Detroit squared off after a brawl erupted over a fight between Gordie Howe and Howie Meeker. Lumley (six foot, 195 pounds), three inches taller and 15 pounds heavier than Broda (five foot nine, 180 pounds), had the clear advantage in size but no winner was declared. Toronto won 4-2.

2.18 B. Hartford's Greg Millen

The first 2,000-shot goalie on record is Greg Millen, who faced 2,056 shots while backstopping 60 Whalers game in 1982-83, the first year shots were officially recorded. Millen averaged 34.3 shots per game, or five shots more each match, than that season's league average of 29.1. A pretty good goalie who had the misfortune of playing behind a feeble defense, Millen went 14-38-6 and produced a dreadful 4.81 goals-against average. Hartford finished the year tied at 45 points with Pittsburgh in the NHL cellar, 65 points behind the league-leading Boston Bruins.

2.19 D. Dominik Hasek

As of 1998-99, among the three netminders (Potvin, Joseph and Hasek) who have faced 2,000 shots in a season three times, only Hasek has recorded three consecutive 2,000-shot seasons. In 1995-96, the Dominator faced 2,011 shots; in 1996-97, 2,177 shots; and in 1997-98, 2,149 shots. During that span the Buffalo Sabres steadily improved their defense in front of Hasek, chopping their shots-against averages of 35.3 shots per game in 1995-96 to 30.6 shots in 1997-98.

2.20 D. Jim Rutherford

Rutherford played on four teams in his 457-game career, three of them after trades in 1980-81 when he stopped for coffee in Detroit for 10 games, Toronto for 18 games and Los Angeles for three games. Rutherford's 31-game season produced a 9-16-4 record and the first team hat trick season for a goalie. As of 1998, three other 400-game goalies have moved three times in a season: Greg Millen guarded the cage for St. Louis, Quebec and Chicago (in 1989-90); Kirk McLean for Vancouver, Carolina and Florida (in 1997-98); and McLean's trading partner, Sean Burke, for Carolina, Vancouver and Philadelphia (in 1997-98).

GAME 2

ROOKIE WONDERS

Since the Calder Trophy was first awarded in 1933, only 13 goalies have been named NHL rookie of the year. In this puzzle, find all 13 puckstoppers by reading across, up, down or diagonally. Like our example of Chicago's Mike K-A-R-A-K-A-S, the league's first Calder-winning netminder, connect the names using letters no more than once. Start with the letters printed in heavy type.

(Solutions are on page 118)

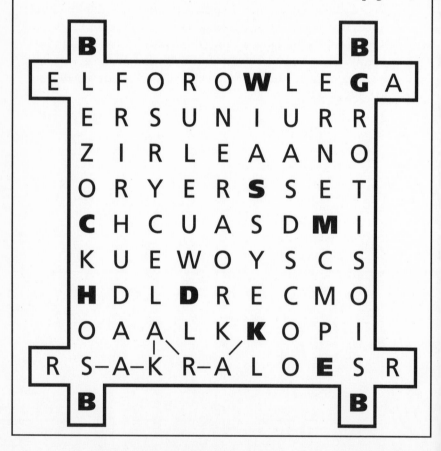

3

PIPE DREAMS

The quality of goalie equipment has increased dramatically since net-minders first began using thin layers of cotton, felt and leather as protection against the puck. Often, goalies themselves have been the innovators. Frank Brimsek, for example, built bamboo ribbing into his stick-side glove and invented the first blocker so that he could stop shots with the back of his hand. Gradually, a rectangular-shaped slab in the glove became the standard, adding protection and, eventually, with the top end angled outward, making it a versatile shield for directing rebounds. In this chapter, we look at goalie equipment and the bumps and bruises of the trade.

(Answers are on page 35)

3.1   Which goalie is known for talking to his goalposts?
A. Ed Belfour
B. Mike Richter
C. Patrick Roy
D. Ron Hextall

3.2   The NHL refused to allow an advertisement for sparkplugs on which goalie's mask during the 1970s?
A. Bernie Parent's
B. Ed Giacomin's
C. Tony Esposito's
D. Gary Smith's

3.3   In what decade did the NHL introduce the goal crease?
A. The 1920s
B. The 1930s
C. The 1940s
D. The 1950s

3.4 Which old-time netminder invented the goaltender's trapper glove?
A. Toronto's Turk Broda
B. Chicago's Emile Francis
C. Detroit's Harry Lumley
D. Montreal's Jacques Plante

3.5 Which goalie once painted stitches on his mask to represent the injuries he might have received?
A. Gerry Cheevers
B. Don Edwards
C. Rogatien Vachon
D. Bob Sauve

3.6 What is the maximum allowable width across a goalie's sweater?
A. 22 inches
B. 26 inches
C. 30 inches
D. 34 inches

3.7 Which NHL goalie switches hands on his stick and fires the puck backhanded out of his own end?
A. Mike Richter
B. Curtis Joseph
C. Nikolai Khabibulin
D. Chris Osgood

3.8 How much time does a goalie have to react to a 90-mile-per-hour shot fired from the blueline?
A. Less than 0.5 seconds
B. Between 0.5 seconds and one second
C. Between one second and 1.5 seconds
D. More than 1.5 seconds

3.9 Why did the NHL conduct an investigation into goalie nets in 1957?
A. To determine the best method for anchoring nets
B. To verify standard net dimensions
C. To prove the netting was puck proof
D. To correct crease size

3.10 Which New York Ranger goalie once wore sweater No. 00?
A. Ed Giacomin
B. John Davidson
C. Mike Richter
D. John Vanbiesbrouck

3.11 Gump Worsley played 21 NHL seasons from 1952 to 1974. In which year did he begin wearing a mask during regular-season games?
A. Gump's 10th season, 1962-63
B. Gump's 15th season, 1967-68
C. Gump's 19th season, 1971-72
D. Gump's last season, 1973-74

3.12 Which goalie always performs this ritual: after catching the puck and before handing it to the referee, he flips the puck into the air so that it lands on the backside of his catching glove?
A. Bill Ranford
B. Martin Brodeur
C. Trevor Kidd
D. Dominik Hasek

3.13 Which goalie is best known for vigorously whacking his stick on both posts in a swinging motion, alternately hitting one post with the blade and the other with the butt end?
A. Garth Snow
B. Curtis Joseph
C. Ron Hextall
D. Bill Ranford

3.14 In what NHL season did a goalie first place his water bottle on top of his net?
A. 1964-65
B. 1974-75
C. 1984-85
D. 1994-95

3.15 Which goalie had his sweater number retired first by an NHL team?
A. Toronto's No. 1, Turk Broda
B. New York's No. 1, Ed Giacomin
C. Montreal's No. 1, Jacques Plante
D. Philadelphia's No. 1, Bernie Parent

3.16 What does goalie Jean-Sebastien Giguere do differently from almost all other goalies when drinking from his water bottle?
A. Giguere spikes his bottle water with a sport drink
B. Giguere chews crushed ice
C. Giguere uses a straw
D. Giguere drinks milk

3.17 Which NHL goalie wears a sweater number that pays tribute to Soviet netminder Vladislav Tretiak?
A. Ed Belfour
B. Nikolai Khabibulin
C. Arturs Irbe
D. Olaf Kolzig

3.18 In which decade did an NHL goaltender first wear a face mask in a regular-season game?
A. The 1920s
B. The 1930s
C. The 1940s
D. The 1950s

3.19 Which goalie invented the butterfly stance?
A. Glenn Hall
B. Tony Esposito
C. Patrick Roy
D. Ed Belfour

3.20 Who is considered the first goalie to have his career extended by switching from regular leg pads to synthetic pads?
A. Bob Sauve
B. Reggie Lemelin
C. Billy Smith
D. Denis Herron

PIPE DREAMS
Answers

3.1 **C. Patrick Roy**
During the 1986 playoffs, in Roy's rookie year, Montreal faced the New York Rangers in the Conference finals. After winning Game 3 in "miraculous" fashion in overtime (13 saves in nine minutes before Claude Lemieux scored the game winner), Roy was asked by New York reporters, "Why did you turn around and stare at your net after the national anthem?" Roy, who spoke very little English at the time, responded, "I was talking to my goalposts." The New York scribes loved the comment and made a big deal out of it, especially after such a spectacular win. When his English improved, Roy explained that he really doesn't talk to his posts. He just looks at the net and creates a vision of the net getting smaller. This gives him more confidence and makes him feel bigger. His inspiration led the Canadiens, a seventh-place overall team, to a surprise Stanley Cup. Roy was named playoff MVP and became an overnight goaltending sensation.

3.2 **B. Ed Giacomin's**
After his trade to the Detroit Red Wings, Giacomin swung a deal with Champion Spark Plugs to carry a "Spark with Eddie"

advertisement on his mask. The league torpedoed the arrangement but Eddie kept the motif he had designed and wore it on his final mask, as a Red Wing.

3.3 B. The 1930s

After decades of playing hockey without a formalized territory for goaltenders, the NHL created an imaginary 10-foot no-screening zone in front of the goal in 1932-33. Then, in 1934-35, an actual crease appeared, eight feet wide and five feet deep, to define the goalie's turf. Painted right on the ice, skaters were forbidden to interfere with netminders in this 40-square-foot area. Throughout the years the crease changed size until, finally, in 1998, it was altered to eight feet wide by four feet six (with a rounded top), almost the same dimensions as first conceived in 1934-35.

3.4 B. Chicago's Emile Francis

Remarkable as it may seem, it wasn't until 1946-47 that the netminding fraternity could claim a suitable catching glove. Goalies wore a regular hockey glove with a piece of leather sewn between the thumb and forefinger on the catching hand. Francis, who played local baseball in Saskatchewan during the off-season, took a Rawlings George McGuinn-model three-finger first baseman's mitt and sewed on a hockey glove gauntlet cuff. His hybrid became the game's first trapper. Soon other netminders followed Francis's lead, adding a completely new dimension to the position.

3.5 A. Gerry Cheevers

Cheevers is considered the first NHL goalie to decorate his face mask. Although less artful than today's customized paint jobs, Cheevers's "fright-night" mask conveyed a simple but dramatic image, that of the battle-scarred warrior. The famous black stitch marks covering his mask date back to 1967-68 when Cheevers was hit by a Fred Stanfield shot at practice. As a joke the scratch on the mask was painted with stitches. By 1971, Cheevers had etched hundreds of stitches on three different masks. His zipper-like motif inspired a trend of self-expression as goalies began to decorate their masks, first with team logos and later with more stylized designs. As the mask evolved in construction to include greater protection to the sides and top of the head, an industry of mask makers and artists developed, producing both safer and more ornate mask designs for goaltenders.

3.6   C. 30 inches

With scoring at an all-time low and goalies using their equipment to full advantage, a number of new rules came into effect in 1998-99. Netminders cannot wear jerseys of more than 29 inches across the chest or 30 inches at the base. There is no limit on length measurement, but a jersey is illegal "if it covers any area between the legs." New rules also disallowed "tying down" of sweaters at the wrists, which creates tension or a "webbing effect" in the armpit area.

3.7   B. Curtis Joseph

Since the 1970s, goaltenders have become more proficient at the transitional game, easing the pressure from opponents by firing the puck directly out of their own zone. Sometimes acting like a third defenseman, one of the best at the long bomb is Curtis Joseph. Because Joseph catches left and shoots right (which is uncommon), to get the puck up-ice he has to catch it with his left hand, drop it to the ice, wheel to his left, put his catching glove at the butt end, swing the stick across his body and get into a backhand shooting stance. The method takes more time to set up but Joseph gets maximum power from the left curve of his blade. When Joseph switches hands like that it's usually a signal for his teammates to move up-ice. The benefit is a defense-to-offense transition that catches the opposition on the forecheck and flat-skated in the neutral zone. As of 1998, Joseph is still looking for his first goal.

3.8   A. Less than 0.5 seconds

A 90 miles-per-hour slap shot fired from the blueline travels to the goal line, 60 feet away, in 0.45 seconds. With such precious little time, goalies coming out 10 feet to cut down the angle have an eye-blink, or just 0.37 seconds, to block the shot. Staying back opens up more net to the shooter but the netminder gains a crucial fraction of a second of reaction time. He is also positioned better for tips and deflections. In that short span of time and at that speed, it's almost impossible to visually follow the puck. So goalies depend on mobility and positioning, using game experience to construct mental trajectories of the shot so they can move into its flight path.

3.9   B. To verify standard net dimensions

Everyone thought Jacques Plante had finally lost it when he said nets varied in size—until measurements were taken. Even though all NHL clubs used official goal nets, Plante believed the nets in Chicago, Boston and New York were lower than the four-foot regulation height. He was soon proven correct. The three NHL rinks had welded the two-inch crossbar to the sides of the posts rather than to the tops, shortening the nets by two inches. Plante noticed the irregularity because the crossbars at these three rinks hit his back in a different place than the crossbars at other rinks.

3.10 B. John Davidson

After Phil Esposito and Ken Hodge began wearing No. 77 and No. 88, respectively, with the Rangers in 1975, Espo convinced Davidson to try double zeroes on his jersey. The idea lasted only one season for Davidson, who was heckled by fans incessantly. He eventually went back to No. 30.

3.11 D. Gump's last season, 1973-74

Gump played maskless for 855 regular-season games and 70 in the postseason before Minnesota's other goalie, Cesare Maniago, convinced him to wear a mask. But Gump did so only in his last six games. Worsley, being the proverbial old dog, claimed he couldn't see the puck at his feet and the mask was too hot. Gump played his last game on April 2, 1974; he was almost 45 years old.

3.12 A. Bill Ranford

Rituals are an athlete's obsession, and players and their teams perform varied and complex routines honed to perfection over years of playing hockey. As you can imagine, goaltenders, often the most eccentric players on the ice, incorporate idiosyncrasies that go beyond their usual housekeeping duties, such as sweeping ice buildup from the front of the crease. For example, Bill Ranford refuses to allow any official to take the puck once he has caught it in his trapper; Ranford has to flip the puck into the air so that it lands on the backside of his catcher. The officials always wait patiently before recovering it, knowing Ranford's behaviour is a part of his game.

3.13 C. Ron Hextall

Much like Ken Dryden's "the thinker" stance during stoppages in play, Hextall has his own particular mannerisms, including one that obviously suits his "take-no-quarter" temperament. In preparation for a face-off Hextall often clangs his stick on both posts in a unique back and forth action, hitting the blade off one post and the butt end off the other.

3.14 C. 1984-85

No exact date is on record, but the water bottle first appeared on top of the net in 1984-85, when the Flyers duo of Bob Froese and Pelle Lindbergh began using the green plastic container during game action. The idea probably originated in the U.S. college ranks. In the pro system, Froese first brought the water bottle out with him stuck on top of the net with velcro. Since no rules were broken, few objected, except Edmonton coach Glen Sather. Smarting after a 4-1 loss to the Flyers in Game 1 of the 1985 Stanley Cup finals, Sather snapped, "What are they going to want up there next, a bucket of chicken?"

3.15 D. Philadelphia's No. 1, Bernie Parent

As of 1998-99, only eight netminders have had their jerseys retired by their NHL teams. Contrary to what one might expect, the first player distinguished wasn't an old-timer like Georges Vezina or Glenn Hall. In fact, the first retired goalie sweater belonged to a post-1967-expansion player. On October 11, 1979, the Philadelphia Flyers retired No. 1, honouring Bernie Parent, who was forced to quit after being struck in the eye with a stick in 1979. In 486 games with the Flyers, Parent had a 232-141-104 record with a 2.42 GAA and 50 shutouts.

Retired Goalie Sweater Numbers*			
Number	**Player**	**Team**	**Date**
No. 1	Bernie Parent	Philadelphia	October 11, 1979
No. 30	Rogie Vachon	Los Angeles	February 14, 1985
No. 1	Glenn Hall	Chicago	November 20, 1988
No. 35	Tony Esposito	Chicago	November 20, 1988
No. 1	Ed Giacomin	NY Rangers	March 15, 1989
No. 31	Billy Smith	NY Islanders	February 20, 1993
No. 1	Terry Sawchuk	Detroit	March 6, 1994
No. 1	Jacques Plante	Montreal	October 7, 1995

Note: *Toronto's Turk Broda and Johnny Bower's No. 1 is an "honoured" (not retired) number and remains in circulation.*
* *Current to 1998*

3.16 C. Giguere uses a straw

Giguere has a rare gastric condition that causes his body to take in too much air when he drinks fluids. As a result, his body has difficulty absorbing water, which, with all the sweating he does during a game, leads to severe dehydration. His problem was so acute that in one AHL game in 1997-98, Giguere lost 19 pounds, became sick and was rushed to hospital. Team doctors in Calgary later discovered the gastric condition that caused his weight loss; Giguere began drinking water from his bottle with a straw to reduce air intake.

3.17 A. Ed Belfour

Belfour wears No. 20 in honour of his most influential goalie coach, Vladislav Trekiak, who began coaching in Chicago in Belfour's rookie season (1990-91). That year, Belfour walked away with all of hockey's top awards for a goaltender. Tretiak never played in the NHL but his famous jersey number endures on the back of his star pupil. Belfour's No. 20 is the lowest double-digit number currently worn by an NHL goalie.

3.18 B. The 1930s

Considered the netminder's single most important piece of equipment today, the goal mask was once regarded as a symbol of cowardice—an impractical device that restricted vision. But in 1959, when Montreal's Jacques Plante slipped on his home-made Fiberglas mask in a game against New York, he changed the face of goaltending forever. Plante's subsequent success opened the door for other goalies. But where Plante got it right, another goalkeeper, 29 years earlier, failed. The distinction of hockey's first mask falls to the Montreal Maroons' Clint Benedict, who wore his face protector in 1930. On January 7, 1930, Benedict was felled by a rising 25-foot blast from Howie Morenz that smashed his nose and cheekbone. "I saw it at the last split second and lunged," Benedict said. "Wham, I was out like a light and woke up in the hospital." A reporter recalled that the puck had "crushed in the side of Benny's face like an eggshell." The injury forced Benedict to use a crude leather mask, modified either from a football face mask (in use at the time) or a boxer's sparring mask. But the contraption didn't work. "The nosepiece protruded too far and obscured my vision on low shots," Benedict said. After a 2-1 loss to Chicago, he threw out the mask and tried a wire cage-type protector, "but the wires distracted me. That's when I gave up." Benedict continued to play maskless, but later that season another Morenz shot struck him in the throat, ending his career. He held no grudges against Morenz. "You know, if we had been able to perfect the mask I could have been a 20-year man." Benedict played 17 seasons and was inducted into the Hockey Hall of Fame in 1965. Despite Benedict's early trials with a face protector, though, it is Plante who usually gets the credit, and deservedly so.

3.19 A. Glenn Hall

Goalies are remembered in many ways: some for their game-winning saves, others for their Stanley Cup victories or their unique personalities. In Glenn Hall's case, he will be forever linked to one of hockey's most important innovations, the inverted-V style, or butterfly stance, which he pioneered long before modern-day practitioners such as Ed Belfour and Patrick Roy. Hall, a lanky six-footer, "got into the butterfly kind of by accident," when the game changed offensively with the slap shot and defensively with more screened shots. Not comfortable with the traditional stance of stand-up goalies, who stayed on their feet and kept their legs together, Hall spaced his feet wide apart and hugged his knees. When he dropped to the ice his knees were together and his legs splayed to either side, forming a wall of pads 10 inches high across the goalmouth. It was a goalie first that few purists endorsed at the time, yet Hall's new crouch-and-drop technique made him faster and more agile post-to-post, and gave him a better view on screen shots. He could also get back on his feet more quickly. It wasn't until the next generation of goalies (including Tony Esposito) that Hall's butterfly was copied. As it turned out, the inverted-V became goaltending's most enduring style.

3.20 B. Reggie Lemelin

In 1986-87, Calgary Flames netminder Reggie Lemelin tried out a pair of synthetic legs pads (made by inventor Jim Lowson) that weighed one-third the weight of his conventional pads. As a result, Lemelin's back problems eased and his career was revitalized. Other netminders also benefited from Lowson's Aeroflex pads, but Lemelin is credited as being the first to wear them.

GAME 3

"I STITCH BETTER WHEN MY SKIN IS SMOOTH"

When asked in 1991-92 if he would rather finish the season with a non-playoff team like San Jose or go back to Kansas City to backstop a contending minor-league team, Sharks goalie Arturs Irbe said, "I would rather be a pauper amongst kings than a king amongst paupers." In this game we look at both the eloquent and not-so-eloquent one-liners from hockey's most quotable stoppers. Match the nine goalies below with their famous quotes. *(Solutions are on page 119)*

Dominik Hasek	Terry Sawchuk	Gilles Gratton
Glenn Hall	Lorne Chabot	Johnny Bower
Gump Worsley	Glenn Resch	John Vanbiesbrouck

1. _____ "In biblical times I stoned people to death. Now they are repaying me by hurling pucks at my head."

2. _____ "I stitch better when my skin is smooth."

3. _____ "Only Dunlop has seen more rubber than I have."

4. _____ "I just made up my mind I was going to lose teeth and have my face cut to pieces. It was easy."

5. _____ "It's the only way I can support my family. If I could do it some other way, I wouldn't be playing goal."

6. _____ "We are the sort of people who make health insurance popular."

7. _____ "Yes, and I also like jumping out of tall buildings."

8. _____ "The only job worse is a javelin catcher at a track-and-field meet."

9. _____ "I want to thank my friends the goalposts for getting me here tonight."

4

ZERO HEROES

Hal Winkler's name and 75-game NHL career will never attract attention in the hockey record books. Nor will he ever be elected to the Hall of Fame. But Winkler will forever be tied to two of hockey's most important shutouts. In his inaugural game on November 16, 1926, Winkler zilched the Montreal Maroons 1-0 to become the first goalie in NHL history to record a shutout in his first career game. Two months later, New York traded him to Boston where, on April 2, 1927, Winkler became part of another historic shutout first. What was it? And who was the other goalie involved? In this chapter get ready to be blanked on questions about both hockey's more obscure and obvious zero heroes.

(Answers are on page 50)

4.1 What is the highest number of shutouts ever recorded by a goalie in one NHL season?
A. 14 shutouts
B. 18 shutouts
C. 22 shutouts
D. 26 shutouts

4.2 In 1953-54, Harry Lumley's 13 shutouts set the *modern-day* record for most zeroes in a season. Who broke that mark to establish the modern-day record?
A. Tony Esposito
B. Ken Dryden
C. Martin Brodeur
D. Dominik Hasek

4.3 Which goalie recorded the highest single-season shutout mark in the 1980s?
A. Grant Fuhr
B. Pete Peeters
C. Mike Liut
D. Tom Barrasso

4.4 Which goalie recorded the most shutouts in the 1990s?
A. Patrick Roy
B. Dominik Hasek
C. Martin Brodeur
D. Ed Belfour

4.5 In November 1926, New York's Hal Winkler became the first goalie in NHL history to record a shutout in his first game. In what other famous shutout first did he participate?
A. Played in the NHL's first 0-0 scoreless game
B. Played in the NHL's first playoff shutout
C. Recorded a shutout in his last NHL game
D. Played opposite the first goalie who recorded a shutout in his first playoff game

4.6 In what year did two goaltenders first share a shutout in regular-season play?
A. 1930-31
B. 1940-41
C. 1950-51
D. 1960-61

4.7 What is the longest shutout stretch by a goalie in regular-season play?
A. Between 200 and 300 minutes
B. Between 300 and 400 minutes
C. Between 400 and 500 minutes
D. More than 500 minutes

4.8 Which old-time netminder did Terry Sawchuk surpass to finally take the lead in NHL career shutouts?
A. Georges Vezina
B. Tiny Thompson
C. Alex Connell
D. George Hainsworth

4.9 Which active goalie of the 1990s has the best (albeit, unrealistic) chance of becoming the NHL's shutout king?
A. Ed Belfour
B. Patrick Roy
C. Dominik Hasek
D. Martin Brodeur

4.10 With which team did Terry Sawchuk, the NHL's shutout king, record his most shutouts?
A. The Detroit Red Wings
B. The Boston Bruins
C. The Toronto Maple Leafs
D. The New York Rangers

4.11 As of 1997-98, what is the most number of shutouts recorded *league-wide* in one NHL season?
A. 75 to 100 shutouts
B. 100 to 125 shutouts
C. 125 to 150 shutouts
D. More than 150 shutouts

4.12 Which old-time goalie was the first NHL netminder to register a double-digit shutout season?
A. Alex Connell
B. George Hainsworth
C. Clint Benedict
D. Roy Worters

4.13 When was the last time two NHL goalies notched double-digit shutout records in the same season?
A. During the 1960s
B. During the 1970s
C. During the 1980s
D. During the 1990s

4.14 Prior to Martin Brodeur recording back-to-back double-digit shutout seasons in 1996-97 (10 shutouts) and 1997-98 (10 shutouts), who was the last goalie to do it?
A. Dominik Hasek
B. Ken Dryden
C. Tony Esposito
D. Bernie Parent

4.15 What is the most number of career shutouts recorded by a goalie in the playoffs?
A. 10 shutouts
B. 15 shutouts
C. 20 shutouts
D. 25 shutouts

4.16 Which nickname did Boston fans give to Frank Brimsek when he posted 10 shutouts in his rookie season of 1938-39?
A. Mr. Zero
B. Brimsek the Blanker
C. Zilch Man
D. Dr. Goose Egg

4.17 When Dominik Hasek collected six shutouts in December 1997, he tied an NHL record from what hockey season?
A. 1928-29
B. 1948-49
C. 1968-69
D. 1988-89

4.18 Which team iced the only netminders in NHL history to record a shutout at an All-Star game?

A. The Toronto Maple Leafs
B. The Detroit Red Wings
C. The Montreal Canadiens
D. The Boston Bruins

4.19 Who is the only goalie to record more shutouts in the playoffs than in regular-season action?

A. Ken Wregget
B. Ron Low
C. Eddie Mio
D. Steve Penney

ZERO HEROES
Answers

4.1 **C. 22 shutouts**

It's with good reason that 1928-29 was the year of the shutout. In that year, players were penalized for a forward pass inside the attacking zone, a rule that only served to emphasize defense. Goalies amassed an astounding 120 shutouts, an extraordinary amount considering that mark was only topped decades later in the defensive trap-oriented years of the 1990s, when the league played twice as many games with more than double the number of teams. While it's rare for a goalie today to register a double-digit shutout season, in 1928-29 eight goalies had 10 or more zeroes to their credit. Montreal's George Hainsworth collected 22 shutouts in the 44-game schedule, an NHL record that still stands and will certainly never be broken.

4.2 **A. Tony Esposito**

In 1969-70 Esposito caught fire and established a modern-day NHL record of 15 shutouts, surpassing Harry Lumley's 16-year mark of 13 zeroes. Esposito posted a 2.17 goals-against average and a 38-17-8 record to lead Chicago to first place overall (only the second time in Blackhawk history). He won the Vezina

Trophy as top puckstopper, the Calder Trophy as rookie of the year and came second only to Bobby Orr in Hart Trophy voting as league MVP. Esposito was a classic overnight success story. His 15 shutouts is an NHL all-time high for rookie goalies from *all* eras.

4.3   B. Pete Peeters

One of the best netminders of the 1980s, Peeters's career began in Philadelphia. He then moved to Boston, where he produced his finest season in 1982-83. Backstopping the Bruins in 62 games, Peeters blanked the opposition eight times and had a 2.36 goals-against average, the best NHL totals in a decade of free-wheeling offense. His 31-game unbeaten streak that year is the second-longest in league history (next to Gerry Cheevers's 32-game run in 1971-72). Peeters also recorded a 27-game undefeated streak with Philadelphia, when the Flyers established an NHL-record 35-game unbeaten streak in 1979-80.

4.4   D. Ed Belfour

Belfour shared or led the league in shutouts four times in the 1990s, compiling 45 shutouts between 1989-90 and 1998-99, just three more than Hasek (42 shutouts), eight more than Patrick Roy (37) and nine more than Brodeur (36).

4.5   D. Played opposite the first goalie who recorded a shutout in his first playoff game

On April 2, 1927, four months after Winkler became the first goalie to notch a shutout in his first career game, he became part of another first when Lorne Chabot of the Rangers earned a shutout against Winkler in a New York-Boston 0-0 tie during the Stanley Cup semifinals. Like Winkler's history-making regular-season shutout debut, Chabot became the first rookie goalie to earn a zero in his first playoff game. Winkler was in goal for both historic shutout firsts. Ironically, during that season Winkler was sent to the Bruins; Chabot replaced him in the New York nets. This means that both Winkler and Chabot played for the same team, the New York Rangers, when they each recorded their landmark rookie shutouts.

4.6   C. 1950-51

Considering that the two-goalie system didn't take hold until the early 1960s, it's understandable that netminders might never have shared a shutout until then. But in 1950-51, the opportunity was ripe as Toronto rotated two regular goalies, veteran Turk Broda and rookie Al Rollins. On December 2, 1950, Rollins sustained a bad cut and was replaced by Broda. Broda stepped in and preserved the zero for the Maple Leafs, marking what is believed the first tandem shutout. Opposing Detroit goalie Harry Lumley didn't fair too badly either, considering he also kept the opposition scoreless. The final tally was 0-0, but the night was rough all round: Lumley suffered a broken nose in the game. (For those trivia kings who suggest the first shared shutout between goalies was on December 5, 1927, when the New York Americans' Normie Himes replaced Joe Miller in a 0-0 tie against the Pittsburgh Pirates, here's a news flash: Himes was a full-time centre on the Amerks, only donning goalie pads because no backup was available.)

4.7   C. Between 400 and 500 minutes

In the era before forward passing was permitted, a number of all-time shutout records were established, including the longest shutout streak. The mark belongs to Ottawa's Alex Connell, who was statistically among the league's best netminders during the 1920s and 1930s. Connell's record shutout sequence began on January 28, 1928, and continued for 446 minutes and nine seconds of hockey. He notched six shutouts in a row, four in overtime. Indicative of that defense-minded era, three games were 0-0 ties.

4.8   D. George Hainsworth

By the time Hainsworth's great hockey career was over in 1937, he had set many of the game's most important shutout records, including most in one season (22) and most in a career (94). With the exception of Alex Connell and Tiny Thompson, few goalies in that era put up such impressive numbers as Hainsworth. In his first three seasons, before forward passing rules were modernized in 1928-29, the Montreal goalie recorded 49 shutouts, more than half of his 11-year career total of 94. Sawchuk, equally impressive early in his career, amassed half his career total of 103 in his first five full seasons with Detroit, bagging 56 zeroes between 1950-51 and 1954-55. The big night in shutout history came on January 18, 1964, 27 years after Hainsworth retired. Sawchuk took over the shutout lead, netting number 95 against, ironically, the Canadiens, Hainsworth's old team. It was a hard-fought 2-0 win. Sawchuk had not shut out the Habs on Montreal Forum ice in eight seasons and the Habs had not lost a game at their own rink in months. With only two minutes left in the game, the Canadiens pulled goalie Charlie Hodge for the extra attacker. In David Dupuis's biography, *Sawchuk*, Red Wing Marcel Pronovost recalls the Canadiens' plan. "I played the last two minutes of that game and when they pulled Hodge, we thought, 'You sons of bitches, you won't give Terry his record, eh? We'll show you.' It only made us all madder and we dug down even deeper." At the final siren, Sawchuk was mobbed by his teammates: the NHL had a new shutout king.

The NHL's All-Time Shutout Leaders

Goalie	MPT*	Years	GP	Shutouts
Terry Sawchuk (1949-1970)	Detroit	21	971	103
George Hainsworth (1926-1937)	Montreal	11	465	94
Glenn Hall (1952-1971)	Chicago	18	906	84
Jacques Plante (1952-1973)	Montreal	18	837	82
Tiny Thompson (1928-1940)	Boston	12	553	81
Alex Connell (1924-1937)	Ottawa	12	417	81
Tony Esposito (1968-1984)	Chicago	16	886	76

Most prominent team

4.9 D. Martin Brodeur
Although Terry Sawchuk's mark of 103 shutouts is virtually unassailable, at least one goalie in the 1990s is making an early case that it could be challenged (but only under better-than-ideal circumstances). Dominik Hasek, Patrick Roy and Ed Belfour are all leading active shutout leaders with 40-plus zeroes heading into the 21st century, but they are too old for serious consideration. The leading candidate has to be Martin Brodeur, who in six short years has amassed 36 shutouts with the New Jersey Devils. A long, healthy career in defense-minded New Jersey could help Brodeur overtake Tony Esposito's 76 shutouts, but never Sawchuk's awesome 103. It's nice to dream though.

4.10 A. The Detroit Red Wings
Sawchuk leads all NHL goalies in shutouts, with 103 zeroes during his legendary 21-year career. His best team record in this category is with Detroit, where he played 734 games and notched 85 shutouts. Sawchuk also manned the pipes for Boston (11 shutouts), Toronto (four shutouts), Los Angeles (two shutouts) and New York (one shutout).

4.11 D. More than 150 shutouts
NHL goaltenders posted record shutout numbers in 1997-98, totalling a whopping 160 shutouts—or about one shutout every 6.5 games! Every NHL team except two notched at least three zeroes, only Calgary and the Rangers failed to get any. Hasek amassed 13 blanks, the best shutout total since Tony Esposito's modern-day record of 15 in 1969-70. Improved conditioning and coaching, bigger equipment and the neutral-zone trap are the main reasons for the shutout surge.

4.12 A. Alex Connell
Connell, an Ottawa fireman before signing with the Senators in 1925, became the first NHL goalie to get 10 or more shutouts in a season in 1925-26. In that sophomore year, he notched an amazing 15 shutouts in the 36-game schedule. Although he led all of his peers in zeroes and goals-against average (1.12) that

season, little comparison can be made to today's backstoppers. With the "no forward passing" rule in effect until 1928, no player could accept a pass from one zone to another. Hockey was often a defensive struggle, so goalies routinely compiled double-digit shutout seasons. To inject more offense into the game, the rule was amended in 1928-29 to include forward passing everywhere except in the attacking zone. Still, during the 44-game schedule, there were 120 shutouts, 95 tied games and a league-wide goals-against average of 2.80. The next season the rules changed again to permit passing in all three zones, yet Connell's play was still exemplary: his career goals-against average of 1.91 ties the renowned George Hainsworth for the lowest mark in NHL history.

4.13 D. During the 1990s

Since 1928-29 it has only happened five times. The most recent was in 1997-98, when Hasek recorded 13 blanks, Brodeur, 10. It marked the first occasion in 24 years that two goalies amassed double-digit shutout totals. Philadelphia's Bernie Parent (12) and Chicago's Tony Esposito (10) did it in 1973-74.

Tandem Double-Digit Shutout Goalies*				
Year	**Goalies**	**Team**	**SO**	**GP**
1932-33	Tiny Thompson	Boston	11	48
	John Roach	Detroit	10	48
1952-53	Gerry McNeil	Montreal	10	70
	Harry Lumley	Toronto	10	70
1953-54	Harry Lumley	Toronto	13	70
	Terry Sawchuk	Detroit	12	70
1973-74	Bernie Parent	Flyers	12	78
	Tony Esposito	Chicago	10	78
1997-98	Dominik Hasek	Buffalo	13	72
	Martin Brodeur	New Jersey	10	70
*Current to 1997-98				

4.14 D. Bernie Parent

Few modern-day netminders have notched consecutive double-digit shutout years. Brodeur accomplished the feat with a pair of 10-shutout years, in 1996-97 and 1997-98. Prior to that, you have to go back to Bernie Parent, who nailed double 12-shutout seasons in 1973-74 and in 1974-75. Esposito recorded two double-digit shutout years, though not consecutively; Dryden only managed one; Hasek, as of 1998, also has one.

4.15 B. 15 shutouts

Although he receives less attention than the great Georges Vezina, Clint Benedict was recognized by players of his era as one of the game's best goalies. During the 1920s, when teams played far fewer games at playoff time than today, Benedict racked up an NHL record 15 shutouts in only 48 postseason matches. He won Stanley Cups with the Ottawa Senators in 1920, 1921 and 1923, and with the Montreal Maroons in 1926. The next-best record is Jacques Plante's 14 zeroes, followed by Turk Broda at 13 and Terry Sawchuk with 12.

4.16 A. Mr. Zero

Brimsek's toughest assignment came in his rookie year as a replacement for 10-year Bruin veteran Tiny Thompson, whom Boston fans adored. In his first game, Brimsek, playing at home, was blanked 2-0 by Montreal—a difficult start in the wake of the past heroics of Thompson. But the next three games changed everything. The rookie came back and notched back-to-back-to-back shutouts and totalled six goose eggs in his first eight games. By the end of the season Boston fans had almost forgotten Thompson. Their new zero hero was Brimsek, who won not only their hearts but the Vezina and Calder Trophies, and, finally, the Stanley Cup. Among all the awards and accolades bestowed on him in that first season, few are remembered more today than the title given him by his fans, Mr. Zero.

4.17 A. 1928-29

Hasek's six shutouts in December 1997 tied the 69-year-old NHL record of George Hainsworth, who notched an unprecedented two six-shutout months in January and February, 1929. Considering most modern goalies don't get six zeroes in a season, never mind in one month, Hasek's feat is remarkable. No goalie had done it in almost 70 years—and when Hainsworth recorded his half-dozen in a month forward passing in the attacking zone was still illegal. Hasek's run began on December 3, when he blanked Anaheim 4-0; then Tampa Bay 4-0 on December 5; Montreal 1-0 on December 19; the Rangers twice, 2-0 on December 21 and 3-0 on December 26; and, finally, Ottawa 3-0 on December 31.

4.18 C. The Montreal Canadiens

Although All-Star games have become high-scoring affairs, at one time they were much tighter contests. In 1967 the defending Cup champions, the Montreal Canadiens, defeated the NHL All-Stars 3-0 in the first and only shutout in All-Star history. Charlie Hodge and backup Gary Bauman shared the goose egg. The game was probably Bauman's greatest moment. In his brief 35-game career, he never once netted a shutout.

4.19 D. Steve Penney

During his 91-game NHL career, Penney logged only one shutout. But in 27 playoff contests for Montreal during the mid-1980s he recorded four zeroes, a league-leading three shutouts, in his rookie postseason (1983-84). Canadiens fans thought they had found the next Ken Dryden, but Penney failed to materialize into the real thing. The following season a new kid, Patrick Roy, was brought up. Thanks to Roy's spectacular play Montreal won the Stanley Cup in 1986. Penney was gone, an afterthought in Roy's wake and the only NHL goalie to net more shutouts in the playoffs than in the regular season.

GAME 4

THE HOCKEY CROSSWORD

(Solutions are on page 119)

Across

1. Paul ____ 1990s Flames/Whalers forward
5. Bryon ____ 1990s Kings/Bruins goalie
8. Opposite of go
10. Boston's Bobby ____
11. To applaud
12. Cam ____ 1990s Hawks D-man
13. Brian ____ 1970-80s Habs/Caps/Kings D-man
14. To attempt
15. Pat "Boxcar" ____ 1940s Bruins
18. Stat: ____ on goal.
20. Glen ____ Oilers boss
21. Referee ____ VanHellemond
23. The Kings' home
24. The Devils' Martin ____
25. The Penguins' Ken ____
29. Iron man goalie Glenn ____
30. Old Isles boss Al ____
33. Frank Brimsek "____ Zero"
34. ____ Broten
35. "The puck ____ the post."
36. Chico ____
39. Dick ____ 1960-70s Leafs/Habs
40. ____ Myre
43. The Leafs' home

44. 1990s backup Chris ____
47. Wealthy
49. Gary ____ 1970s Bruins D-man
50. "____ ethic"
52. "The game is broadcast ____ from MSG."
54. ____ Belfour
55. Arturs ____
56. Bruins great Derek ____
57. ____ Clapper, 1940s Bruins D-man

Down

1. The Rangers' Mike ____
2. Ex-Bruins power forward Cam ____
3. Bob ____ 1980-90s Pens/six-team winger
4. Andy ____ Oilers/Bruins/Stars goalie
5. Practice workout
6. To ____ a lineup.
7. Bob ____ Jets/Oilers goalie
8. Tim ____ Wings/Jets goalie
9. Ex-Canuck Kirk ____
16. Brothers Frank and Pete ____
17. Bobby ____ 1970s journeyman
19. The game ends, it's ____.
22. The Penguins' Tom ____

58

24. Montreal coach Toe ____
26. Mike ____ Caps/Rangers/Leafs 500-goal man
27. Toronto's ____ Broda
28. Most NHLer's favourite summer sport
31. Detroit ____ Wings
32. Bob ____ 1940s Bruins star
33. 1980s Olympic "____ on Ice"
36. Ottawa's Damian ____
37. Ankle injury
38. To strike a player
41. Prying bar
42. ____ Jordon
45. Todd ____ 1990s Habs/Ducks enforcer
46. The Flyers' ____ Brind'Amour
48. Hello
51. Detroit's Trevor ____ D
53. "Make him ____ his words."

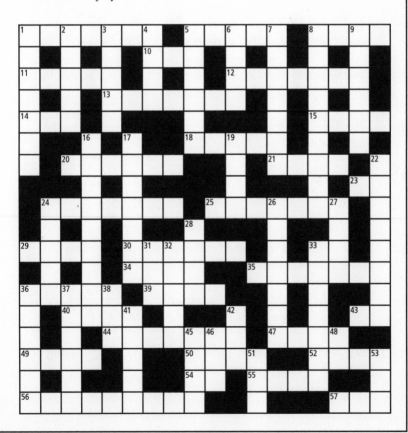

59

5

TRUE OR FALSE?

The most successful brother goalies in the NHL were Ken and Dave Dryden. Although Ken played in 397 games and Dave in 203 games, the brothers never opposed each other in NHL action: true or false? In this chapter we take a break from multiple-choice queries and settle a few scores on topics of a true-or-false nature in the goaltending brotherhood.

(Answers are on page 62)

5.1 Most goalies follow the same routine when dressing: left skate, right skate, left pad, right pad. *True or False?*

5.2 Tony Esposito's first goal-against in the NHL was scored by brother Phil Esposito. *True or False?*

5.3 Terry Sawchuk recorded his 200th win as a member of the Detroit Red Wings. *True or False?*

5.4 Until Grant Fuhr joined St. Louis in 1995-96, he had never had a regular-season goals-against average below 3.00. *True or False?*

5.5 As of 1997-98, Dominik Hasek had recorded all of his 33 career shutouts with Buffalo. *True or False?*

5.6 Glenn Hall's only game misconduct occurred during his first NHL game using a goalie mask. *True or False?*

5.7 No goalie ever won the Hart Trophy as MVP while playing on a last-place team. *True or False?*

5.8 The only NHL game Boston goalie Dave Reece played in came on the night he allowed Toronto's Darryl Sittler to score a league-record six goals and 10 points. *True or False?*

5.9 For many years during his NHL career Ron Hextall had more goals than shutouts. *True or False?*

5.10 As of 1997-98, Sean Burke hadn't allowed a goal on a penalty shot. *True or False?*

5.11 Jacques Plante retired from professional hockey two times. *True or False?*

5.12 Tom Barrasso is the only goalie to jump directly from high school to the NHL. *True or False?*

5.13 A goalie was the first American-born NHLer inducted into the Hockey Hall of Fame. *True or False?*

5.14 Patrick Roy is the only goalie in NHL history to give up more than one sniper's 500th career goal. *True or False?*

5.15 Despite being hockey's most successful brother goalies, Ken and Dave Dryden never played opposite each other in the NHL? *True or False?*

5.16 Since 1967, no Stanley Cup final series ever featured two starting goaltenders who were previously traded for each other. *True or False?*

5.17 John Vanbiesbrouck has the longest surname in the history of NHL goaltenders. *True or False?*

5.18 No team has ever had two 30-win goalies in one season. *True or False?*

5.19 Vladislav Tretiak is the first Soviet-trained player elected to the Hockey Hall of Fame. *True or False?*

5.20 Although Terry Sawchuk leads the NHL in career shutouts, with 103, he does not hold the record for single-team career shutouts. *True or False?*

5.21 Every goalie who won the Hart Trophy as league MVP also claimed, at one time or another, the Vezina Trophy as top netminder. *True or False?*

5.22 Billy Smith is the first professional goalie credited with scoring a goal in a regular-season game. *True or False?*

5.23 Ken Dryden is the only player to win the Stanley Cup prior to capturing the Calder Trophy as top rookie. *True or False?*

TRUE OR FALSE?
Answers

5.1 True

Although no official survey substantiates this claim, it's considered a fact that most big-league goalies lace up their left skate and then their right, followed by their left and right pads.

5.2 True

A goal is a goal, no matter who's in nets. Phil had little sympathy for his kid brother, Tony, who, in his first NHL game on December 5, 1969, was scored upon twice by the elder Esposito in a Montreal-Boston 2-2 tie. Esposito, filling in for an injured Rogatien Vachon and a nerve-wracked Gump Worsley, blocked 33 shots for the tie. "What's the big idea?" Tony asked Phil after the game. "It's bad enough that you got one goal, but two—that's ridiculous." It was the first time in more than 30 years that a brother shot against another brother in NHL play.

5.3 False

After five straight seasons of leading the league in victories, Sawchuk, with 199 wins, was traded by Detroit to Boston in 1955. His 200th victory came on October 12, 1955, in a 2-0 Bruins win over Toronto. It was Sawchuk's 58th career shutout.

5.4 True

In his first 14 NHL seasons, Fuhr never managed an average below 3.00, either with Glen Sather's run-and-gun Stanley Cup winners of the 1980s nor with Toronto, Buffalo or Los Angeles. Only when Fuhr joined Mike Keenan's Blues in 1995-96 did his goals-against come down. In three successive seasons, Fuhr recorded averages of 2.87, 2.72 and 2.53, the best of his distinguished career.

5.5 False

Hasek played 25 games and notched one shutout with the Chicago Blackhawks, his first NHL team, before being traded to Buffalo in 1992.

5.6 True

The only time Hall was tossed from an NHL game was on November 13, 1968, the night the goalie marvel wore his first mask. Rarely at ease before any game, Hall was especially nervous on that critical evening. Almost immediately, the St. Louis netminder gave up a 60-footer to New York's Vic Hatfield. Then, after Blues defenseman Noel Picard was penalized, Hall flicked his glove at referee Vern Buffey in protest, connecting with the official's shoulder. After just two minutes of play the masked Hall was ejected, the only game misconduct in his 18-year NHL career. Afterwards, Hall joked, "Well, every time I wear a mask I get thrown out of the game."

5.7 False

In fact, two NHLers have won MVP status while playing with cellar dwellers: Brooklyn Americans defenseman Tommy Anderson in 1942 and goalie Al Rollins of the Chicago Blackhawks in 1954. The Hawks finished last in the six-team NHL while Rollins managed a 3.23 goals-against average, worst in the league among starters that season. Rollins's 47 losses that season stood as an NHL record until Gary Smith passed him with 48 losses in 1970-71.

5.8 False

In fact, Reece had already played in 13 other games, recording a surprising two shutouts before that fateful night. Sittler's record 10-point game was Reece's undoing. He never backstopped another NHL contest.

5.9 True

In his first five NHL seasons, Hextall's record stood at two goals and just one shutout.

5.10 True

Sean Burke blanked all five of the shooters he faced in penalty-shot confrontations prior to 1998-99.

5.11 False

Plante, who is best remembered for helping Montreal win six Stanley Cups in the 1950s, played on five other professional teams and officially retired three times. The first time he quit was in 1965, after 10 seasons with Montreal and two with the New York Rangers. He came back in 1968 after expansion to play five seasons with St. Louis, Toronto and Boston. He retired again just in time for another hockey expansion, the NHL's rival league, the WHA. Plante played 31 games with the Edmonton Oilers in 1974-75, his last pro season and third retirement year after three decades of hockey.

5.12 True

Although Bobby Carpenter was the first player to jump from high school to the NHL, the first netminder was Barrasso, who one day was playing high school hockey in Acton-Boxboro, Massachusetts, and only a few months later with Scotty Bowman's Buffalo Sabres. Selected fifth overall in the 1983 draft, Barrasso, just 18 years old, proved to be one of Bowman's most astute picks ever: he won the NHL's best rookie and top goaltending awards in 1983-84, and later backstopped Pittsburgh to consecutive Stanley Cups in 1991 and 1992. As of March 1999, Barrasso is still the only goalie to go directly from high school to the NHL.

5.13 True

The first U.S.-born NHLer elected to the Hockey Hall of Fame was Boston Bruins goalie great Frank Brimsek of Eveleth, Minnesota. Although Brimsek was inducted in 1966, three other Americans preceded him into the Hall, but none were NHLers. Hobey Baker was inducted in 1945, Si Griffis in 1950 and Frank "Moose" Goheen in 1952.

5.14 True

As of 1998, only Roy had two 500th goals-against credits. Roy, who is among the top three goalies in most games played during the 1990s, gave up Steve Yzerman's 500th on January 17, 1996, then Joe Mullen's 500th on March 14, 1997. Three of the 27 500th goals scored in NHL action have gone into empty nets.

5.15 False

Brother netminders are rare. In fact, the Drydens are the only siblings to play at the NHL level in more than 100 games each. Combined, the brothers worked 778 regular-season and playoff matches, but only six times against each other. When they faced each other as opposing goalies for the first time in a Montreal-Buffalo game at the Montreal Forum on March 20, 1971, it was a landmark occasion in league history. Both were backups in the game, but when Ken subbed for an injured Rogatien Vachon, Sabres coach Punch Imlach pulled Joe Daley to let Dave play opposite Ken. The Forum fans were thrilled. After the 5-2 Canadiens win, the two Drydens skated to centre ice and, in a regular-season oddity, shook hands. Dave and Ken played five more times against each other, including twice during the 1973 playoffs, another NHL first. For the record, Ken won three, lost one and tied two against his big brother.

5.16 False

At the 1988 Entry Draft, Boston and Edmonton exchanged goalies Bill Ranford and Andy Moog, who two years later battled each other in the Oilers-Bruins 1990 Stanley Cup finals. The goaltender's duel turned into hockey history in the first game as Moog and Ranford protected a 2-2 tie until 55:13 of overtime. The marathon match represented the longest game in Stanley Cup finals play. Moog faced 31 shots in the 3-2 loss; Ranford, who had been beaten twice in the third period by Ray Bourque to force overtime, kicked out everything else in his 52-shot effort. Backstopped by Ranford's spectacular play, the Oilers whipped the Bruins 4-1 in the best-of-seven series. Ranford won the Conn Smythe Trophy as playoff MVP.

5.17 True
Vanbiesbrouck's surname is 13 letters long, the longest in league annals. It tops Peter Sidorkiewicz's name by only one letter. The shortest name? Plenty of stoppers have three-letter names, including Eddie Mio, Ron Low and Patrick Roy.

5.18 True
In order for two goalies on the same team to each record 30-win seasons, their club has to win at least 60 games. Only two teams (both coached by Scotty Bowman) have ever achieved the 60-win mark: the 1976-77 Montreal Canadiens (60 wins) and the 1995-96 Detroit Red Wings (62 wins). Neither club on these occasions split the goaltending duties equally between their respective netminders: the Canadiens' Ken Dryden won 41 games in 1976-77 and Chris Osgood racked up 39 Detroit victories in 1995-96. The closest any tandem goalies came to a 30-30 season was in 1983-84, when Edmonton's Grant Fuhr (30 wins) and Andy Moog (27 wins) combined for 57 victories.

5.19 True
Tretiak, one of the best goalies of all time and certainly the greatest netminder ever produced by the Soviet Union, was inducted into the Hockey Hall of Fame in 1989, the first Soviet player so honoured.

5.20 False
Of his 103 career shutouts, Sawchuk recorded 85 with Detroit —10 more than the next-highest single-team mark of 75, netted by Montreal's George Hainsworth.

5.21 False

Among the five goalies to win league MVP honours (Roy Worters, Chuck Rayner, Al Rollins, Jacques Plante and Dominik Hasek), only Rayner (MVP in 1950) never earned a Vezina. Instead, Rayner spent much of his career stopping pucks for last-place teams such as the New York Americans and, later, the Rangers.

5.22 False

Although Smith was credited with a goal in November 1979, he wasn't the first pro goalie to score. On February 21, 1971, Michel Plasse, playing for Kansas City in the Central Hockey League, scored when the opposing goalie for Oklahoma was removed for an extra attacker. Plasse maintains to this day that he wasn't trying to score, just to clear the puck out of his zone. As of 1998, 22 goalies have scored a total of 24 times in the top North American leagues.

5.23 False

Four players have won the Stanley Cup before they won the Calder. Habs goalie Ken Dryden may be the most famous; he captured the Cup in 1971 and rookie of the year honours in 1972. But three others proceeded him: Danny Grant won a championship ring with Montreal in 1968 and the Calder in 1969 as a Minnesota North Star; Tony Esposito, who played backup goalie with the 1969 Cup-winning Canadiens and then recorded 15 shutouts for Chicago the following season as top rookie; and Gaye Stewart, the first Cup winner to earn the Calder (in 1942 and 1943).

GAME 5

NET WORTH

Among the many trophies presented to individuals each year in the NHL, one of the most prestigious was originally donated by Maple Leaf Gardens. In the award's brief history, only nine netminders have distinguished themselves by winning the prize. Unscramble the goalie's names by placing each letter in the correct order in the boxes. Then unscramble the letters in the circled boxes to spell out the three-word name of our mysterious award.

(Solutions are on page 120)

A L H L

ONVERN

Y R O

DRANFRO

LAXTHEL

T M I H S

RNYDNE

EZRIORC

TNREPA

6

ICONS OF THE ORIGINAL SIX

From 1942 to 1967, the NHL iced a six-team league that produced many of hockey's greatest netminders. The Sawchuks, Halls and Plantes still dot the record books, but records alone do not capture these goalies' profound effect on the sport. Terry Sawchuk's crouch, Glenn Hall's butterfly and Jacques Plante's mask all influenced the next generation of puckstoppers and those who followed them between the posts. Some of their feats remain unduplicated, such as the longevity of Gump Worsley and Terry Sawchuk, goaltending's only 20-year men. In this chapter we celebrate the golden age of the Original Six, when many were ready but only a few were called.

(Answers are on page 73)

6.1   Which Original Six netminder is considered to be the most scarred goalie?
  A. Jacques Plante
  B. Johnny Bower
  C. Glenn Hall
  D. Terry Sawchuk

6.2   Which netminder from the six-team era was known as the China Wall?
  A. Bill Durnan
  B. Johnny Bower
  C. Terry Sawchuk
  D. Charlie Hodge

6.3   How long is Glenn Hall's consecutive-games record?
  A. 200 to 300 games
  B. 300 to 400 games
  C. 400 to 500 games
  D. More than 500 games

6.4 Who was Chicago's backup goalie during Glenn Hall's consecutive-games streak?
A. Al Rollins
B. Denis Dejordy
C. Henry Bassen
D. Harry Lumley

6.5 In 1951-52, NHL goalies experienced one of their most injury-free seasons. How many starting goalies in the six-team NHL played the entire 70-game schedule?
A. Three goalies
B. Four goalies
C. Five goalies
D. Six goalies

6.6 For which unusual physical characteristic was Montreal goalie Bill Durnan known in the 1940s?
A. He was nearsighted and wore glasses
B. He had a trick knee that regularily popped out
C. He was ambidextrous
D. He had a metal plate in his head

6.7 Which Original Six netminder's actions forced the NHL to introduce a rule in 1959-60 that penalized a goaltender for leaving his crease to freeze the puck?
A. Jacques Plante's
B. Emile Francis's
C. Gump Worsley's
D. Connie Dion's

6.8 The youngest goalie to play an NHL game came from the six-team era. How old was he?
A. 15 years old
B. 16 years old
C. 17 years old
D. 18 years old

6.9 Which Original Six goalie holds the NHL career record for all-time wins?
A. Terry Sawchuk
B. Glenn Hall
C. Jacques Plante
D. Johnny Bower

6.10 Which goalie from the six-team era is the only Calder Trophy winner (top rookie) in NHL history to miss the entire season after winning the trophy?
A. Toronto's Frank McCool (in 1945)
B. New York's Gump Worsley (in 1953)
C. Detroit's Glenn Hall (in 1956)
D. Detroit's Roger Crozier (in 1965)

6.11 Which Original Six goalie is famous for attempting to score goals?
A. Johnny Bower
B. Sugar Jim Henry
C. Bill Durnan
D. Charlie Rayner

6.12 Who or what were "the pirates" in the nickname "Terry and the Pirates?"
A. Terry Sawchuk's fan club
B. Terry Sawchuk's defense corps
C. Terry Sawchuk's old equipment bag
D. Terry Sawchuk's drinking buddies

6.13 Which Vezina Trophy-winning goalie first requested that his partner's name also be inscribed on the award?
A. Glenn Hall
B. Don Simmons
C. Terry Sawchuk
D. Johnny Bower

6.14 What pair of netminders formed the NHL's first two-goaltender system?
A. New York's Chuck Rayner and Emile Francis
B. Toronto's Turk Broda and Al Rollins
C. Montreal's Gerry McNeil and Jacques Plante
D. Detroit's Harry Lumley and Connie Dion

6.15 Which Original Six netminder has appeared in the most playoff games and series in Stanley Cup finals history?
A. Glenn Hall
B. Terry Sawchuk
C. Turk Broda
D. Jacques Plante

6.16 Which Hall of Fame goalie did the Montreal Canadiens receive in a seven-player trade that dealt away the famed Jacques Plante?
A. Charlie Hodge
B. Gump Worsley
C. Rogie Vachon
D. Tony Esposito

6.17 Where did Lorne Worsley's nickname "Gump" come from?
A. A cartoon character
B. A family relative
C. A movie star
D. An ex-goalie

6.18 Which Original Six netminder first played in 100 career playoff games?
A. Jacques Plante
B. Bill Durnan
C. Turk Broda
D. Glenn Hall

6.19 Which excuse did Glenn Hall use to avoid training camp each fall?
  A. He was painting his barn
  B. He had a groin pull
  C. He was writing his memoirs
  D. He was being fitted for new pads

ICONS OF THE ORIGINAL SIX
Answers

6.1   D. Terry Sawchuk
Because most goalies of the six-team era only donned masks in the 1960s (and some waited until the early 1970s), they often averaged upwards of 200 stitches on their faces by the time they retired. Terry Sawchuk may be the exception. Before he wore his first mask in 1962, Sawchuk needed 400 stitches to sew up his face, including three in his right eyeball. In 1966, *Look* magazine photographed Sawchuk's patchwork of scars. Through effective lighting and a make-up artist's enhancement of the stitchwork, Sawchuk projected an almost grotesque image, disfigured with facial dents, sunken eyes and blackened zipper-like stitches. Scarier, and more real, than any Halloween mask, the photo shocked millions of magazine readers.

6.2   B. Johnny Bower
Like the ancient architectural marvel in China after which he was nicknamed, Bower's presence was formidable. He was the classic stand-up goalie who, while receiving few accolades, faithfully guarded his territory longer than any of his contemporaries. When Bower made the NHL in 1958-59, he was already regarded a veteran, after, as he said, "13 years riding the bus" in the AHL. His long road to glory was through Cleveland, where he laboured eight seasons as a star-in-waiting, winning multiple top goalie awards, MVP honours and a slew of All-Star appearances. In 1953-54, Bower backstopped the struggling New York Rangers, a team that won only 29 games, yet he recorded five shutouts and a goals-against average of 2.60 while

playing in all 70 games. Shipped back to Cleveland (and Providence), Bower played just seven NHL games in the next three years before Punch Imlach's Maple Leafs came calling. It was his first real opportunity at the NHL and Bower was almost 34 years old. Defying age, the old pro proved instrumental in rejuvenating the Leafs, winning the Vezina Trophy as top goalie twice and the Stanley Cup four times during the next 11 seasons. Bower retired in 1969-70 at 45. Immovable, almost irreplaceable, he really was the China Wall.

6.3   **D. More than 500 games**
Before the two-goalie system, clubs in the six-team NHL often counted on their goalies to play entire seasons without missing a game. Some netminders managed to complete the gruelling 70-game schedule, but no one matched the consistency of Hall—he played continuously for seven seasons from 1955-56 to 1961-62, a total of 502 straight games. Hall's astonishing ironman streak earned him the Rookie of the Year Award in 1956, the Stanley Cup in 1961 and six All-Star berths. His stretch ended on November 7, 1962. He had strained his back at practice while fastening a toe strap. The next night, midway through the first period, the pain was so severe that Hall removed himself from play.

6.4   **B. Denis Dejordy**
Like Bobby Hull, Pierre Pilote and other young, talented juniors, Dejordy came from Chicago's farm team, the St. Catherines Teepees of the Ontario Hockey League. Dejordy joined the Teepees in Glenn Hall's first year as a Blackhawk, 1957-58, but unlike Hall, who made the NHL club immediately, Dejordy waited out Hall's streak over five seasons before playing his first NHL game. Like Pilote before him, Dejordy honed his skills with the Hawks' affiliate in the American Hockey League, the Buffalo Bisons (and also with the EPHL's Sault St. Marie Thunderbirds). During that time he led his respective leagues in wins four times and in shutouts twice. But as long as Hall was healthy in Chicago, Dejordy was little more than long-distance injury insurance in the one-goalie system of the six-team NHL.

The long wait for Dejordy finally ended in November 1962, when a back problem forced Hall out of a game against Boston. Dejordy replaced him (in a 3-3 tie against the Bruins) and played two nights later in Montreal (a 3-1 win over the Canadiens), ending Hall's amazing ironman record. Over the next two seasons Dejordy played just 11 games and didn't get any consistent NHL action until 1964-65, when he managed 30 games as Hall's regular backup. By that time Dejordy had spent seven seasons in wait. He was already in his prime at age 26.

6.5 C. Five goalies

New York's Chuck Rayner was the only goalie among all six starters to suffer an injury severe enough to sideline him for an extended period; he played in 53 games before being replaced by Emile Francis. The five other regulars, Terry Sawchuk, Al Rollins, Gerry McNeil, Sugar Jim Henry and Harry Lumley, all completed their team's 70-game schedules in 1951-52.

6.6 C. He was ambidextrous

Durnan, one of the best goalies in the 1940s, wore specially constructed gloves that were both stick and catching mitts, enabling him to switch his stick from hand to hand depending on the shooter. In *A Breed Apart*, author Douglas Hunter quotes Detroit's Normie Smith: "Normally, a goalie's good side is where he catches the puck. Because he can catch with either hand, Durnan is equally good on either side of the net. Watch him, and you will find that when a puck carrier comes in on the right wing, Durnan will switch his stick to his left side of the net. Then he can catch the puck with his right hand on the big side of the net, and vice versa. Unlike other players he doesn't use the posts much in shifting about. Instead he glides back and forth." As Hunter points out, goalie Davey Kerr of New York was also ambidextrous, "but never so flamboyant" as Durnan.

6.7 A. Jacques Plante's

Plante was instrumental in so many changes to hockey, only he could be responsible for such a rule. Until he entered the league most goalies remained in their creases. Plante's habit of roaming the ice to stop the puck for his defensemen or pass it up-ice to his forwards was considered radical, yet for the Canadiens it produced smoother, faster transitions in their game. But when the Montreal netminder got caught out of position he would deliberately smother the puck to force a stoppage in play. Unfortunately, Plante used the trick even when the opposition was pressing on the attack. After numerous complaints, the NHL created Rule 55, preventing goalies from falling on the puck outside the crease.

6.8 C. 17 years old

Harry Lumley's Hall of Fame career began during World War II on December 22, 1943, when the Detroit Red Wings called up the 17-year-old rookie from Indianapolis for a two-game trial. Lumley got blown out by Chicago 7-1, an inauspicious start for the future NHL star. But he played again the next night, though not for the Red Wings. After his dismal performance, Detroit regular Norman Smith was back in nets facing the Rangers. In the third period New York goalie Ken McAuley suffered an injury and without a spare goalie on the bench, the Rangers borrowed the 17-year-old kid from Detroit. Playing against his own team, Lumley lost again 5-3. His rookie start was brief but he always knew why he was there. "Because there was such a shortage of players, I made it," Lumley once said, recalling the lean war years. Within two seasons he became Detroit's number one starter. Lumley is still the youngest goalie to play in an NHL game.

6.9 A. Terry Sawchuk

Few goalies can rival the longevity of Sawchuk, who still holds a number of NHL records, including most career wins. Sawchuk won 447 games; Plante squeaks into second with 434 wins; and Tony Esposito, the most recent goalie to challenge Sawchuk's crown, has 423 victories. In postseason action Sawchuk adds another 54 wins for a grand total of 501 career wins.

6.10 B. New York's Gump Worsley (in 1953)

Worsley got what he thought was his big break after the Rangers' Charlie Rayner suffered a career-ending knee injury in 1952. The raw rookie, fresh from the Saskatoon farm team, backstopped the weak New York team for the last 50 games of 1952-53, winning the Calder Trophy as top rookie with a 13-29-8 record. But when he asked for a $500 raise the next season, Worsley found himself in the WHL with Vancouver. "Everybody thinks Johnny Bower beat me out of a job but it had to be the money," says Worsley in Dick Irvin's book, *In the Crease.* "The next year, Camille Henry won the rookie award with the Rangers and he asked for a $500 raise. I got news for you: he ended up in Providence for most of the year." The celebrated Ranger centre, though healthy, didn't play a full NHL season until 1957-58. Such was the NHL during the six-team era.

6.11 D. Charlie Rayner

Rayner's ambition was to score a goal in the NHL. His penchant for playing the point on a delayed penalty put him in good position on numerous occasions. On January 2, 1947, the Rangers goalie raced up the ice to Toronto's blueline with 35 seconds remaining to assist in tying a 5-4 game. Then, on January 25, while defending a 1-0 shutout (with the Maple Leafs' Turk Broda on the bench for the extra attacker), Rayner dashed 30 feet for a loose puck in the dying seconds and fired the puck up-ice, barely missing the empty net. Against the Canadiens on February 1, Rayner made several dashes into Montreal's zone to try and score the equalizer while trailing 2-1 late in the game. In 1950, he failed again in an opportunity to become the league's first goal-scoring goalie. In the last minute of play, with Toronto trying to get the equalizer, Rayner blocked a shot and, instead of clearing it to the side, banked a shot off the boards that slid down the ice and just missed the vacated net. Rayner never scored in NHL action but his dream did come true while playing with his Rangers teammates on a barnstorming tour through the Canadian Maritimes in 1951. Facing the Maritime Senior League All-Stars, Rayner deked out the defense and tucked a pretty backhander into the net.

6.12 B. Terry Sawchuk's defense corps

Sawchuk and his five Red Wing defensemen earned the comic strip nickname in the early 1950s, when Detroit was in the midst of winning seven straight league titles and four Stanley Cups. "The Pirates," who so effectively shut down opposing attackers, were his defensemen: Red Kelly, Marcel Pronovost, Leo Reise, Bob Goldham and Benny Woit. Every season the press took a photo of the group and called it "Terry and the Pirates." The original comic strip by the same name was created by Milton Caniss of the *New York Daily News* in the 1930s.

6.13 C. Terry Sawchuk

When Toronto finished 1964-65 with the best goals-against average in the NHL, Sawchuk was automatically awarded the Vezina Trophy because he had played 36 games compared to partner Johnny Bower's 34. In a gesture of true sportsmanship, Sawchuk pointed out that Bower deserved the Vezina, considering he had shut out Detroit 4-0 in the last game of the season to claim the award by a small margin over Red Wing goalie Roger Crozier. As Sawchuk said, "There's the guy who won it. They can put Bower's name on it." In fact, Bower, with 2.38, had a better average than Sawchuk's 2.56. The league agreed and for the first time the Vezina became a joint award. (Today, the best-average goalies are awarded the Jennings Trophy. The Vezina goes to the goalie adjudged best at his position as voted by the general managers of all clubs.)

6.14 B. Toronto's Turk Broda and Al Rollins

Although the NHL's two-goalie rule wasn't introduced until 1965, some teams were pairing netminders (if only for a season or two) years earlier. Toronto tried tandems first in 1950-51, with veteran Turk Broda and rookie Al Rollins sharing duties during the regular season and postseason. The duo clicked as Broda went 14-11-5 in 31 games and Rollins 27-5-8 in 40 matches. In the postseason Rollins and Broda led the Maple Leafs to the Stanley Cup, defeating Montreal in a classic Cup confrontation. But the next season, when Broda retired, Toronto used Rollins exclusively without a backup. Despite Toronto's success, NHL managers (the stingy lot they were) still argued it was better to keep a goalie sharp in the minors than have him lose his edge sitting on an NHL bench. The turning point came during the 1964 playoffs, when Detroit was forced to use minor-leaguer Bob Champoux in nets after Terry Sawchuk suffered an injury. The Red Wings still defeated Chicago 5-4, but using a raw recruit in playoff action drew considerable attention. The next season the NHL adopted the two-goalie system, finally ending the days of long delays waiting for an injured goalie to recuperate or for a house goalie to be pulled from the stands as a sub.

6.15 D. Jacques Plante

Plante's longevity in the Stanley Cup finals is unparalleled: he played in three decades of hockey with Cup finalists from 1953 to 1970. The Montreal netminder worked an NHL record eight straight finals, beginning in 1953 (his rookie season), and then two more years in 1969 and 1970 during his second hockey career with Glenn Hall of St. Louis. In 10 postseasons in the finals, Plante started a record 41 games, won 25 and lost 14. No goalie in playoff action has more wins (25) in the finals than Plante.

6.16 B. Gump Worsley

In a blockbuster trade with New York, Montreal dealt their multiple Vezina Trophy-winning goalie, the ever-temperamental Plante, to the Rangers (with Donny Marshall and Phil Goyette) for Gump Worsley (and Dave Balon, Leon Rochefort and Len Ronson). For Worsley, it was a new beginning after years of suffering on inept Ranger teams. For Plante, it was a big demotion. He played 98 games over the next two seasons before retiring. Meanwhile, in Montreal, Worsley and Charlie Hodge were winning Stanley Cups. After expansion in 1967, Plante was lured back between the pipes to play for St. Louis, Toronto and Boston before his second NHL retirement in 1973. Worsley hung up the pads a year later in 1974 as a Minnesota North Star. Both goalies began their NHL careers in 1952-53.

6.17 A. A cartoon character
Worsley acquired the nickname "Gump" when a childhood friend began comparing him to Andy Gump, a cartoon character that bore a striking resemblance to the rotund goalie and his flat-top brush cut.

6.18 C. Turk Broda
Broda became the first netminder in NHL history to play in 100 postseason games on March 27, 1952, when he faced Detroit in a 1-0 loss in Game 2 of the Stanley Cup semifinals. Broda played just one more playoff game, two nights later in a 6-2 loss—again to the Red Wings. It was a disappointing end to the distinguished career of one of hockey's best money goalies. While Broda iced a solid 2.53 career goals-against average in regular-season play, he wasted the opposition in the playoffs with a sparkling 1.98 average, a 60-39 win-loss record and five Stanley Cups.

6.19 A. He was painting his barn
For years Hall had a reputation for missing training camp, claiming he had to stay home in Stoney Plain, Alberta, and paint his barn. One fall, Scotty Bowman, coach of the St. Louis Blues, visited Hall to have him sign a contract. Dick Irvin's *In the Crease* picks up Scotty's story: "We arrived and he (Hall) was sitting on the front step drinking a beer. We looked around for the famous barn but there wasn't one. We never did see one. As far as I know, he didn't have a barn."

GAME 6

PICK OF THE PACK

Since the NHL Amateur Draft began in 1969, no goalie has ever been chosen first overall. A few, such as Martin Brodeur and Tom Barrasso, have been selected in the first round, but most often they go later, due to the unpredictability of junior or college netminders. Others, like Jon Casey, never get picked but sign as free agents after playing U.S. college hockey. Match the goalies on the right and their draft positions or free agent signings on the left. Use the draft year and team in the left column as clues to help you.

(Solutions are on page 120)

	Overall Pick	Year—Team	Player
1. ____	5th	1983—Buffalo	A. Bill Ranford
2. ____	8th	1981—Edmonton	B. John Vanbiesbrouck
3. ____	20th	1990—New Jersey	C. Ed Belfour
4. ____	24th	1985—New Jersey	D. Andy Moog
5. ____	28th	1985—Rangers	E. Felix Potvin
6. ____	31st	1990—Toronto	F. Martin Brodeur
7. ____	51st	1984—Montreal	G. Tom Barrasso
8. ____	52nd	1985—Boson	H. Curtis Joseph
9. ____	72nd	1981—Rangers	I. Grant Fuhr
10. ____	107th	1984—New Jersey	J. Dominik Hasek
11. ____	119th	1982—Philadelphia	K. Sean Burke
12. ____	132nd	1980—Edmonton	L. Kirk McLean
13. ____	199th	1983—Chicago	M. Mike Richter
14. ____	Free agent	1987—Chicago	N. Ron Hextall
15. ____	Free agent	1989—St. Louis	O. Patrick Roy

7

THE SHOOTING GALLERY

Which goalie faced the most shots in one game? Or recorded the most penalty-shot saves? How about the rookie with the longest win streak? Who has given up the fewest goals? In this chapter we check out the records of many of the game's best backstoppers: those elite players whose statistics remain unequalled.

(Answers are on page 86)

7.1 What is the highest number of wins in a season by a goalie? Name the netminder.
A. 39 wins—Martin Brodeur
B. 43 wins—Tom Barrasso
C. 47 wins—Bernie Parent
D. 51 wins—Grant Fuhr

7.2 What is the highest number of shots faced by a goalie in an NHL game in regulation time (60 minutes)?
A. Between 50 and 60 shots on goal
B. Between 60 and 70 shots on goal
C. Between 70 and 80 shots on goal
D. More than 80 shots on goal

7.3 Which modern-day goalie faced the most shots in a game (in regulation time) without losing?
A. Mike Richter
B. Ron Tugnutt
C. Craig Billington
D. Mike Liut

7.4 What is the greatest number of shots on goal by two teams in one NHL game?
A. Between 90 and 110 shots on goal
B. Between 110 and 130 shots on goal
C. Between 130 and 150 shots on goal
D. More than 150 shots on goal

7.5 As of 1998-99, who faced the most shots in an NHL season?
A. St. Louis' Curtis Joseph in 1993-94
B. Edmonton's Bill Ranford in 1993-94
C. Toronto's Felix Potvin in 1996-97
D. Buffalo's Dominik Hasek in 1997-98

7.6 What is the highest number of shots faced by a goalie in a game (including overtime)?
A. Between 80 and 90 shots on goal
B. Between 90 and 100 shots on goal
C. Between 100 and 110 shots on goal
D. More than 110 shots on goal

7.7 Who holds the NHL record for most games played in one season?
A. Ed Belfour in 1990-91
B. Grant Fuhr in 1995-96
C. Martin Brodeur in 1995-96
D. Felix Potvin in 1996-97

7.8 Since Terry Sawchuk's magical 44-win season in his rookie year, 1950-51, what modern-day goalie has the next-best record for most rookie wins?
A. Chicago's Tony Esposito (in 1969-70)
B. Montreal's Ken Dryden (in 1971-72)
C. Philadelphia's Ron Hextall (in 1986-87)
D. Chicago's Ed Belfour (in 1990-91)

7.9   If the NHL record for the longest undefeated streak by a goalie
      in one season is 32 games, what is the same record for a rookie
      netminder?
      A. 19 games
      B. 23 games
      C. 27 games
      D. 31 games

7.10 What is the record for most penalty shots faced in one
      season?
      A. Three penalty shots
      B. Four penalty shots
      C. Five penalty shots
      D. Six penalty shots

7.11 Which goalie has faced the most penalty shots since 1983-84?
      A. Kelly Hrudey
      B. Patrick Roy
      C. John Vanbiesbrouck
      D. Tom Barrasso

7.12 Which goalie faced the most penalty shots and gave up the
      fewest goals between 1983-84 and 1997-98?
      A. John Vanbiesbrouck
      B. Don Beaupre
      C. Mike Richter
      D. Bill Ranford

7.13 In 346 penalty shots between 1983-84 and 1997-98, how
      many times have goalies stopped a penalty shot in a game in
      which they recorded a shutout?
      A. Less than 10 times
      B. 10 to 30 times
      C. 30 to 60 times
      D. More than 60 times

7.14 Since expansion in 1967, what is the goalie record for leading
the NHL in wins?
A. Two seasons
B. Four seasons
C. Six seasons
D. Eight seasons

7.15 What is the record for points by an NHL goalie in one game?
A. One point
B. Two points
C. Three points
D. Four points

7.16 In 1998-99, which veteran goalie passed Grant Fuhr to lead
all goalies in career scoring points?
A. Curtis Joseph
B. Mike Vernon
C. Ron Hextall
D. Tom Barrasso

7.17 Before Tom Barrasso became the American goalie with the
most wins in NHL history, which old-time netminder held that
title?
A. Sam Lopresti
B. Frank Brimsek
C. Mike Karakas
D. Jack McCartan

7.18 What NHL goalie recorded the most wins during the 1990s?
A. Ed Belfour
B. Mike Richter
C. Mike Vernon
D. Patrick Roy

7.19 What is the most regular-season games played by an NHL goalie who has never appeared in a playoff game?

A. Between 150 and 200 games

B. Between 200 and 250 games

C. Between 250 and 300 games

D. More than 300 games

THE SHOOTING GALLERY
Answers

7.1 **C.** **47 wins—Bernie Parent**

No goalie in NHL history recorded as many wins in a single season as Philadelphia's Bernie Parent in 1973-74, when the Flyers racked up a 50-16-12 season. After seven average seasons, including one year in the WHA, Parent caught fire and won an astonishing 47 games to smash the 22-year record set by Terry Sawchuk (44 wins) in 1951-52. Parent's 47-victory campaign included 12 shutouts, a miserly 1.89 goals-against average and Vezina Trophy honours as top netminder (shared with Tony Esposito of Chicago).

7.2 **D.** **More than 80 shots on goal**

On March 4, 1941, Chicago goalie Sam LoPresti stepped between the pipes and faced a league record 83 shots. Despite stopping 80 shots against Boston marksmen, LoPresti still lost the game as his lacklustre teammates failed to score more than two goals in the 3-2 Bruins win.

7.3 **B.** **Ron Tugnutt**

Fifty years after Chicago's Sam LoPresti was peppered with a record 83 shots in a 3-2 Bruins victory in March 1941, Ron Tugnutt of the Quebec Nordiques faced 73 shots to become the second-busiest goalie in one night of NHL hockey. In Tugnutt's case the struggling Nordiques knotted the Bruins 3-3, providing Tugnutt with the distinction of not losing a game with the greatest shots against. Perhaps Tugnutt's best save came with eight seconds remaining in overtime off a Ray Bourque slap shot.

With Cam Neely in Tugnutt's face at the edge of the crease, Tugnutt did the splits and snatched the rising slapper to preserve the tie. Both Bruin stars skated away shaking their heads. After the game, in an unusual gesture for regular-season play, several Boston players skated across the ice to shake Tugnutt's hand. The game, played on March 21, 1991, was in the same Boston Garden as LoPresti's historic loss a half-century earlier.

7.4   C. Between 130 and 150 shots on goal
On December 26, 1925, two defunct NHL teams, the Pittsburgh Pirates and New York Americans, combined to fire a record 141 shots at goalies Roy Worters of the Pirates and Jake Forbes of the Americans. Worters faced 73 shots against Forbes's 68 in the 3-1 New York victory.

7.5   C. Toronto's Felix Potvin in 1996-97
Since shots against became an official statistic in 1982-83, a number of goalies have held the most shots-on-goal title only to have their mark broken the following season either by themselves or another puckstopper. Since Greg Millen's 2,056 shots in 1982-83, Grant Fuhr, Bob Essensa and Curtis Joseph have all been topped, establishing new milestones in the rain of rubber. As of 1998-99, the most shell-shocked goalie is Felix Potvin, who faced 2,438 shots or 34.2 shots per game in 1996-97 with the Maple Leafs.

Evolution of Shots-Against Milestones					
Player	**Team**	**Season**	**GP/Mins**	**SA**	**SAPG**
Greg Millen	Hartford	1982-83	60/3520	2,056	35.0
Grant Fuhr	Edmonton	1987-88	75/4304	2,066	28.8
Bob Essensa	Winnipeg	1992-93	67/3855	2,119	33.0
Curtis Joseph	St. Louis	1992-93	68/3890	2,202	34.0
Curtis Joseph	St. Louis	1993-94	71/4127	2,382	34.6
Felix Potvin	Toronto	1996-97	74/4271	2,438	34.2

SA/Shots against, SAPG/Shots against per game

7.6 B. Between 90 and 100 shots on goal

No other goalie in NHL history faced as many shots in one game as Detroit netminder Normie Smith. On March 24 and 25, 1936, Smith stood on his head and stopped a record 92 shots from Montreal Maroon snipers in a contest of endurance that went 116:30 in overtime and ended at 2:25 a.m., five hours and 51 minutes after the opening face-off. It was the longest game in NHL history, won on Mud Bruneteau's famous goal at 16:30 of the sixth overtime period. Smith shut the door on the Maroons for 176 minutes and 30 seconds of play. He allowed no goals on 92 shots in the 1-0 win.

7.7 B. Grant Fuhr in 1995-96

Fuhr backstopped Mike Keenan's St. Louis Blues in a league-record 79 games in 1995-96, his first season with the Blues after signing as a free agent in July 1995. Keenan rescued Fuhr's career as a backup in Los Angeles, Buffalo and Toronto by making the 14-year veteran his number one starter. During 1995-96 Fuhr battled with the Devils' Martin Brodeur in the games-played statistical category. In the test of endurance each survived the gruelling schedule, but after 82 games Fuhr had a two-game edge: 79 matches to Brodeur's 77. Yet despite having played two more games, Fuhr logged 4,365 minutes—68 minutes fewer than Brodeur's season total of 4,433, which earned the Devils goalie the new league record for most *minutes* played in a season.

7.8 D. Chicago's Ed Belfour (in 1990-91)

A number of freshman netminders have challenged Sawchuk's 44-win rookie season of 1950-51. Tony Esposito recorded 38 rookie wins in 1969-70, Ken Dryden topped that with 39 in 1971-72 and Hextall had 37 in 1986-87. But Belfour struck the closest in 1990-91, recording 43 rookie wins with Chicago—just one win short of Sawchuk's awesome mark.

7.9 C. 27 games

Boston's Gerry Cheevers owns the league record with a 32-game undefeated streak (24W-8T) in 1971-72, but among rookie netminders, Philadelphia's Pete Peeters strung together the longest stretch without a loss in 1979-80. Peeters went undefeated in 27 games as the Flyers set their own NHL record: a 35-game unbeaten streak. (Some hockey guides refer to Grant Fuhr's 23-game streak in 1981-82 as the longest freshman span, but clearly Peeters edges Fuhr in this category. At issue may be the fact that Peeters played five games in 1978-79, his first season, but not his rookie season.)

7.10 B. Four penalty shots

If it's the exception to face two penalty shots in one season, then a three-shot year is a rarity for NHL netminders. In 15 seasons between 1983-84 and 1997-98, four goalies (Corrado Micalef in 1985-86, Doug Keans in 1987-88, Bill Ranford in 1991-92 and Ed Belfour in 1993-94) faced three penalty shots. But no one in that time (and likely in any other NHL season) can match Toronto's Allan Bester in 1988-89 when he went mano a mano four times with shooters, stoning each one of them, including one to protect a shutout. Bester, playing on a pretty desperate Maple Leaf team (28-46-6), blanked Dino Ciccarelli of Minnesota (November 26, 1988), Michel Goulet of Quebec (December 29, 1988), Greg Adams of Vancouver (January 9, 1989) and Anton Stastny of Quebec (March 7, 1989). In his 219-game NHL career Bester faced only one other penalty shot, keeping his perfect record intact with a stop on Dennis Maruk, December 23, 1986.

7.11 A. Kelly Hrudey

There were 346 penalty shots called during regular-season action from 1983-84 to 1997-98. In that period Hrudey went one-on-one with shooters 12 times, the highest penalty shot count among all netminders. Hrudey stopped six shots and gave up six goals for a 50 per cent success rate, which is just below the league save rate of 59 per cent. In that 15-year span, goalies stopped almost three of every five calls, allowing 141 goals on 346 penalty shots. Hrudey's six goals-against, including two by Mario Lemieux, came in his first seven penalty shots; in the next five shots Hrudey was a perfect 5-0 in shots blocked.

Hrudey robbed the best, including Sergei Fedorov, Mats Sundin and Pavel Bure. Vanbiesbrouck and Roy each faced the next-highest total: nine penalty shots.

7.12 D. Bill Ranford

In any shootout, Ranford has to be the man to go to. In 15 seasons between 1983-84 and 1997-98 he faced nine penalty shots and stopped eight of them, three alone in 1991-92. The lone goal on Ranford was scored by Calgary's Robert Reichel on February 7, 1994, in a 4-3 Edmonton loss to the Flames. In eight penalty shots, Beaupre has stopped shooters six times; Richter, six of seven occasions; and Vanbiesbrouck, five of nine times.

7.13 A. Less than 10 times

In 346 penalty-shot situations in 15 seasons, only nine goalies have preserved shutouts by blanking their shooter.

Penalty Shot Saves that Preserved Shutouts*

Goalie	Team	Shooter	Score	Date
Doug Kearns	Bos	Steve Yzerman	1-0	11/22/87
Allen Bester	Tor	Greg Adams	3-0	1/09/89
Bob Essensa	Wpg	Mike Craig	2-0	1/21/91
Bill Ranford	Edm	Greg Adams	7-0	12/01/91
Darcy Wakaluk	Min	Dave Andreychuk	2-0	2/07/92
John Casey	Min	Luc Robitaille	3-0	4/03/93
Don Beaupre	Ott	Mark Recchi	3-0	2/06/95
Daren Puppa	TB	Doug Weight	5-0	1/03/96
Corey Schwab	TB	Steve Heinze	2-0	12/17/97

Current to 1997-98

7.14 B. Four seasons

Although it's rare in today's game to see a goalie lead the NHL in wins multiple times during his career, it was possible to do it in the six-team era and earlier when only a handful of goalies dominated the league. During the 1920s, 1930s and 1940s, Clint Benedict topped the NHL in wins six seasons; Tiny Thompson five times. In the 1950s and 1960s, Terry Sawchuk and Jacques Plante each managed season wins five times; Glenn Hall and Ed Giacomin three times. In the 1970s, Ken Dryden led or shared the lead in the win column on four occasions; Bernie Parent three times. In the 1980s and 1990s, Patrick Roy and Grant Fuhr have reached most season wins twice.

7.15 C. Three points

Jeff Reese didn't become a household name during his 172-game NHL career, yet his moniker is firmly ensconced in the league record book for his performance on February 10, 1993, when the Calgary Flames annihilated the San Jose Sharks 13-1 and Reese picked up a record three assists.

7.16 D. Tom Barrasso

Throughout much of his career Grant Fuhr topped all goaltenders in offensive numbers. As of 1997-98, he still held his "scoring" lead, established early in his career when he amassed an NHL-record 14 points with Edmonton in 1983-84. In that year he collected more points than 13 of his Oiler teammates! But in 1998-99, his 46-point career mark was challenged and passed by Tom Barrasso who, with 45 points, took over the lead by notching three points (all assists) to Fuhr's zero total that season. Heading into the millennium Barrasso had 48 career points and Fuhr 46.

7.17 B. Frank Brimsek

Brimsek's route to the NHL began in his hometown of Eveleth, Minnesota, where he played high school hockey (before turning amateur in Pittsburgh and pro in New Haven and Providence). Brimsek went on to become Boston's Mr. Zero by twice recording streaks of three consecutive shutouts during his first month of NHL action in 1938. With the exception of Patrick Roy, few goalies have produced such stellar rookie seasons. He led the league in shutouts (10) and goals against (1.56), won the Calder as top rookie and the Vezina as best goalie, and was a selection to the First All-Star Team and the Stanley Cup in 1938-39. By the time he retired in 1950, Brimsek had collected

252 victories, the most by an American-born goalie. Brimsek was certainly the exception. Remarkably, it took another 44 years before Tom Barrasso surpassed Brimsek's U.S. mark, scoring his 253rd victory on February 15, 1994.

7.18 D. Patrick Roy

Roy was far and away the hottest goalie of the 1990s, recording 310 wins in Montreal and Colorado from 1989-90 to 1998-99. Roy's best season was in 1996-97, when he won a league-leading 38 games for the Avalanche. His least productive year was 1994-95, when St. Patrick won only 17 matches as a Canadien. Roy leads all goalkeepers in games played with 591, just ahead of Bill Ranford and Kirk McLean, the only netminders in 1990's top 10 to lose more games than they won.

Player	Team	GP	Wins	Losses	Ties
Patrick Roy	Mtl/Col	591	310	192	72
Ed Belfour	Chi/SJ/Dal	527	272	162	82
Curtis Joseph	St.L/Edm/Tor	524	248	196	61
Mike Vernon	Cal/Det/SJ	482	232	174	67
Mike Richter	NYR	192	230	174	57
John Vanbiesbrouck	NYR/Fla/Phi	510	214	194	81
Andy Moog	Bos/Dal/Mtl	431	207	140	59
Bill Ranford	Edm/Bos/Wash	551	199	244	67
Ron Hextall	Phi/Que/NYI	416	199	143	50
Kirk McLean	Van/Car/Fla	478	197	198	61

The Top 10 Winningest Goalies of the 1990s*

* *Current to 1999*

7.19 C. Between 250 and 300 games

Dunc Wilson logged 287 games with five NHL teams between 1969-70 and 1978-79, and never once appeared in a playoff match. Each of his five clubs—Philadelphia, Vancouver, Toronto, New York and Pittsburgh—were among the worst in the NHL during Wilson's time with each club. When his teams did make the playoffs, such as Toronto in 1974 and Pittsburgh in 1977, Wilson sat on the bench, watching in frustration as his clubs were eliminated.

GAME 7

LAST LINE OF DEFENSE

In this game, the names of the 27 goaltenders listed below appear in the puzzle horizontally, vertically or backwards. Some are quickly found, like Tony E-S-P-O-S-I-T-O; others require a more careful search. After you have circled all 27 names, read the remaining letters in descending order to spell what all of these goalies have in common.

BELFOUR	BOWER	CAREY	DRYDEN	DURNAN
EDWARDS	ESPOSITO	FUHR	GIACOMIN	HAINSWORTH
HALL	HASEK	HERRON	HEXTALL	LAROCQUE
LIUT	PEETERS	PLANTE	PUPPA	ROY
SAWCHUK	SEVIGNY	SMITH	VACHON	VILLEMURE
VANBIESBROUCK		WORSLEY		

(Solutions are on page 121)

```
E R U M E L L I V V E Z V
I U N A L L A T X E H A C
N O H C A V T D U R N A N
E F R A O R E W O B R O Y
D L T U I L P L I E H G O
Y E Y W P N A E Y E I T Y
R B F U H R S E D A I N N
D I P T O B L W C S G O E
H P I C R S A O O I R L T
A M Q O R R M P V R N L N
S U U O D I S E E N T A A
E C W S N E S H E R S H L
K U H C W A S R E T E E P
```

8

MASKS OF SORROW

On December 11, 1985, Edmonton's Grant Fuhr and Chicago's Murray Bannerman and Bob Sauve made hockey history by equalling one of the NHL's longest-standing offensive team records: a 14-7 goal feast in 1919-20, between Toronto and Montreal. That infamous mark stood unchallenged for more than six decades, until 1985 when Bannerman-Sauve and Fuhr gave up a mind-numbing 21 goals in the Oilers' 12-9 decision over the Blackhawks. In all, 62 points were tallied between the clubs, another team record. In this chapter, we bring new meaning to the word "offensive" to describe the following netminding nightmares.

(Answers are on page 98)

8.1 Which Washington goalie was responsible for the most goals against in one NHL season?
   A. Ron Low
   B. Bernie Wolfe
   C. Jim Bedard
   D. Michel Belhumeur

8.2 What is the most losses amassed by a goalie in a single NHL season? (Hint: He did it in a 78-game schedule.)
   A. 38 losses
   B. 48 losses
   C. 58 losses
   D. 68 losses

8.3 Against which former teammate did Wayne Gretzky score his record-breaking career point?
   A. Andy Moog
   B. Bill Ranford
   C. Kelly Hrudey
   D. Grant Fuhr

8.4   What is the highest number of goals allowed by a goalie whose NHL career lasted just one game?
A. Eight goals
B. 10 goals
C. 12 goals
D. 14 goals

8.5   What is longest suspension handed out to Ron Hextall?
A. Three games
B. Six games
C. Nine games
D. 12 games

8.6   Gary Edwards backstopped six NHL teams. What is the least amount of ice time Edwards logged for one club in one season?
A. Four seconds
B. Four minutes
C. Four periods
D. Four games

8.7   The two most famous goals allowed by Gary Edwards may be Guy Lafleur's first goal and Bobby Orr's last. But Edwards also allowed which other memorable goal (or point)?
A. Mike Bossy's record-setting 53rd rookie goal
B. Gordie Howe's last career point
C. Wayne Gretzky's first 50th goal
D. Peter Stastny's record-setting 109th rookie point

8.8   Goalie Lorne Anderson played only three NHL games during the 1950s, but his name is still in the record books for what feat?
A. Most goals against in one game
B. Most penalty minutes by a goalie in one game
C. Allowing the fastest hat trick in NHL history
D. All of the above

8.9 Which goalie suffered the most losses in his career?
A. Gump Worsley
B. Terry Sawchuk
C. Gilles Meloche
D. Glenn Hall

8.10 What is the NHL record for the fastest two goals by one player in the playoffs? Name the goalie.
A. Five seconds
B. 15 seconds
C. 25 seconds
D. 35 seconds

8.11 What is the highest number of games played by an NHL goalie who failed to record one shutout during his career?
A. Between 100 and 120 games
B. Between 120 and 140 games
C. Between 140 and 160 games
D. More than 160 games

8.12 What is the greatest number of games played by an NHL goalie who registered only one career shutout?
A. 50 to 100 games
B. 100 to 150 games
C. 150 to 200 games
D. More than 200 games

8.13 What is the highest number of goals allowed by one netminder in a career? (Name the goalie, too.)
A. 1,700 to 2,000 goals
B. 2,000 to 2,300 goals
C. 2,300 to 2,600 goals
D. More than 2,600 goals

8.14 Against which Montreal netminder did Mario Lemieux score his 545th career goal to surpass ex-Canadiens great Maurice Richard's 544-goal career mark?

A. Patrick Roy

B. Pat Jablonski

C. Jocelyn Thibault

D. Jose Theodore

8.15 Wayne Gretzky scored his 500th career goal into an empty Vancouver net. Which Vancouver netminder was pulled for the extra attacker, resulting in that famous goal?

A. Richard Brodeur

B. John Garrett

C. Troy Gamble

D. Kirk McLean

8.16 In nine penalty shots on Patrick Roy between 1983-84 and 1997-98, how many goals had Roy allowed?

A. Roy stopped all the shots

B. Roy allowed two goals on nine shots

C. Roy allowed four goals on nine shots

D. Roy allowed six goals on nine shots

8.17 The record for most goals allowed by one team in one period of NHL play is nine. What is the same record in the minor pro league, the AHL?

A. Eight goals

B. 10 goals

C. 12 goals

D. 14 goals

8.18 What is the greatest number of 50th goals allowed by a goalie?

A. Four 50th goals

B. Six 50th goals

C. Eight 50th goals

D. Ten 50th goals

8.19 **What is the briefest career of a goalie in the** NHL?
A. Three seconds
B. Three minutes
C. Three periods
D. Three games

MASKS OF SORROW
Answers

8.1 **A. Ron Low**
How bad were the Capitals in their inaugural season? Worse in goals against than the 1992-93 Ottawa Senators and San Jose Sharks, two other first-year teams that own some of the NHL's most embarrassing records. For instance, San Jose and Ottawa rank one-two in most losses in one season (71 and 70 losses), several more than the Capitals' 1974-75 mark of 67. But although their dismal performances may be comparable, considering Washington's 67-loss season occurred in an 80-game schedule and the Senators and Sharks played 84 games to register 71 and 70 losses, the Caps are untouchable in goals allowed. Their 446 goals against that season is a league record. (The 1985-86 Detroit Red Wings are second with 415.) No single Capitals player was responsible, but Low bore the brunt of the punishment, allowing 235 goals in 48 games for a dreadful 5.45 goals-against average. Backup Michel Belhumeur played in 35 games and recorded 162 goals against and a 5.36 average.

8.2 **B. 48 losses**
Gary "Suitcase" Smith may best be remembered as the journeyman goalie who played on a record eight teams, but his 15-year career featured another sorry feat: most losses (48) in a season by a netminder. Smith's undressing happened in 1970-71 while playing for the California Seals, an awful team (20-53-5) with the league's most porous defense and lifeless offense. Smith grew so frustrated with his club's performance that during one game, he tried to score a goal himself on opposition goalie Ed Giacomin of the Rangers. Smith took off for the New York end

and crossed centre ice before being stopped by Rod Seiling, the last Ranger back. Had Smith been able to deke Seiling, he would have had a remarkable breakaway, a one-on-one goalie versus goalie shootout.

The NHL's Top Single-Season Losing Goalies*

Player	Team	Season	GP	Losses
Gary Smith	California	1970-71	71	48
Al Rollins	Chicago	1953-54	66	47
Peter Sidorkiewicz	Ottawa	1992-93	64	46
Harry Lumley	Chicago	1951-52	70	44
Harry Lumley	Chicago	1950-51	64	41
Craig Billington	Ottawa	1993-94	63	41

*Current to 1998-99

8.3   B. Bill Ranford

Months before Wayne Gretzky was traded to Los Angeles in 1988, Edmonton sent Andy Moog to Boston in return for Bill Ranford (and Geoff Courtnall). Ranford, who played just six regular-season games with Gretzky in Edmonton, was back-stopping the Oilers the night the Kings came to town and the Great One scored point number 1,851 to break Gordie Howe's career mark. Gretzky flipped a pass from Dave Taylor over Ranford's shoulder for the historic marker.

8.4   B. 10 goals

What number of games have more goalies played in their career than any other number? One game. Discounting the position players, trainers, coaches and practice goalies who replaced injured or penalized netminders in hockey's early days, some 60 goalies have had one-game careers in the NHL. They either filled in as temporary replacements for a night or for a period or were called up as legitimate tryouts. Among those one-game wonders, Ron Loustel allowed an unprecedented 10 goals in one game for the Winnipeg Jets in 1980-81. The worst goals-against average belongs to Jim Stewart, who made his debut with the Boston Bruins on January 10, 1980. Stewart allowed three goals in the first four minutes and two before the period ended. He was yanked after 20 minutes and five goals with a humbling 15.00 goals-against average. Neither Stewart nor Loustel ever played in the NHL again.

8.5 D. 12 games
Hextall has defended his crease and teammates more vigorously and with more menace than any other goalie in recent memory. His competitive aggressiveness became one of his trademarks, as he laid out victims and piled up penalties; his rap sheet includes three suspensions of six, eight and 12 games. Hextall's bad-boy reputation was established during his rookie season, 1986-87, when he logged a record 104 penalty minutes. Then, in the Stanley Cup finals that season, Hextall felled Edmonton's Kent Nilsson with a wicked slash to the back of his legs that earned Hextall an eight-game suspension in his sophomore year. In 1989-90, he missed Philadelphia's first 12 games for attacking Chris Chelios of the Montreal Canadiens with his blocker in 1989's Wales Conference final. His third-longest suspension was a six-gamer in 1991-92, for slashing Detroit's Jim Cummins in a preseason game.

8.6 B. Four minutes
In his first three pro seasons, Edwards moved between the St. Louis Blues, the Kansas City Blues and San Diego Gulls of the CHL six times, the shortest stay lasting four minutes during one game with St. Louis in 1968-69.

8.7 C. Wayne Gretzky's first 50th goal
During Edwards's 286-game NHL career he gave up 973 goals. Among the three most noteworthy are Guy Lafleur's first, Bobby Orr's last and Wayne Gretzky's first 50th, scored on April 2, 1980, in a Minnesota-Edmonton 1-1 tie.

8.8 C. Allowing the fastest hat trick in NHL history
On March 23, 1952, fate (in the form of Chicago's Bill Mosienko) met Lorne Anderson and cast a humiliating blow. In only his third NHL contest, Anderson was scored upon three

times by Mosienko in a record 21 seconds. Anderson never recovered from the quickest hat trick in league annals; his NHL career ended with a win and two losses. Yet despite his short career, Anderson's shot at the big time did bring him notoriety in the record books, though not for an accomplishment he might have wished for.

8.9 A. Gump Worsley

Although the Gumper won four Stanley Cups late in his career with the powerhouse Montreal Canadiens of the 1960s, he paid his dues during the 1950s with some terrible New York Rangers teams. His rise from "duck in a shooting gallery" to Cup champion produced two completely opposite NHL records. No goalie in league history has been defeated more often (352 losses) than Worsley, yet he holds the game's lowest career goals-against average in Stanley Cup finals action: 1.82 in 16 games. Gilles Meloche, who never won a Cup, has 351 losses, just one less than Worsley. Among active goalies in the 1990s, John Vanbiesbrouck tops the list with 303 losses.

8.10 A. Five seconds

Detroit's Norm Ullman blasted the two fastest playoff goals ever on April 11, 1965, against Glenn Hall of Chicago. Ullman scored at 17:35 and 17:40 of the second period in the fifth game of the semifinals. Detroit won 4-2 but lost the playoff round to the Blackhawks.

8.11 B. Between 120 and 140 games

Pokey Reddick has the longest shutout-less career in NHL annals. He played 132 games with Winnipeg, Edmonton and Florida between 1986-87 and 1993-94, without registering a single zero.

8.12 D. More than 200 games

No other NHL goalie has recorded so few shutouts in so many games as John Garrett. Although a few—Bob Mason (145 games), Kari Takko (142 games) and Frank Pietrangelo (141 games)—are up there, Garrett holds the ignoble honour of recording only one blank in 207 games. It came on March 2, 1983, in a Vancouver win over Winnipeg. "We won 3-0 and Tiger Williams went out after the game (with the trainer's scissors) and cut out a piece of the net for me. The Winnipeg arena crew wasn't too happy about that," recalled Garrett.

8.13 D. More than 2,600 goals
The leading candidates for the distinction of hockey's "most scored upon" are some of the sport's best puckstoppers. Typically, they either played a consistently good game with bad or mediocre teams or, through longevity, acquired a higher goals-against count. The winner (or loser, depending on your viewpoint) is Gilles Meloche. Meloche's 2,756 goals in 18 NHL seasons outdistances all other netminders, but the statistic is deceiving. Meloche, like many in this category, was better than most of the teams he backstopped, including the California Seals and Cleveland Barons. When the Barons merged with Minnesota, Meloche had his finest hour tending the nets in the 1981 Stanley Cup finals against the New York Islanders.

8.14 C. Jocelyn Thibault
It could not have been more appropriate: Montreal-born Mario Lemieux, the NHL's great French-Canadian superstar, surpassed the Rocket's illustrious 544-goal mark with his 545th (against the Canadiens' Thibault) before an ecstatic hometown crowd at the Montreal Forum.

8.15 C. Troy Gamble
The Great One scored number 500 into an empty net on November 22, 1986. Looking on helplessly from the bench was Troy Gamble, who, after allowing four goals (two by Gretzky himself), was pulled for the extra attacker. In the final minute Gretzky squeezed the shot home, bulging the net for the 500th time. Edmonton beat the Canucks 5-2. It was Gamble's first NHL game.

8.16 D. Roy allowed six goals on nine shots

In 15 years, Roy stopped only three shots on nine penalty-shot attempts, a save average of 33 per cent, well below the NHL norm of 59 per cent (141 goals on 346 penalty shots) during that timespan.

8.17 B. 10 goals

In a November 1998 game against the Providence Bruins, Syracuse Crunch goalies Mike Valley and Craig Hillier gave up a combined 10 goals in one period to break the previous nine-goal record set 50 years earlier by the 1947 Pittsburgh Hornets (tied three times since). Valley started the game, let in two quick goals and was pulled just 2:14 into the match. Hillier, a Pittsburgh Penguin prospect from the Ottawa 67s, stepped into the breech. Three minutes later, at 5:23, Providence held a 6-0 lead, better than an average of one goal per minute. By 17:25 Hillier gave up four more markers and Valley was brought back into the nightmare. He held Providence scoreless until the period was over, putting an end to the worst period in AHL annals. Valley then settled down but Providence prevailed 14-2 over Syracuse.

8.18 B. Six 50th goals

Most veteran netminders have allowed a couple of 50th goals in their careers. The exception may be Denis Herron, who in 14 seasons was smoked six times on 50th goals, including a hat trick of 50th markers by Guy Lafleur in 1975, 1976 and 1979, when he backstopped Pittsburgh and Kansas City. Then, in 1984 and 1985, again in Pittsburgh, Herron fell victim on three more occasions to 50th goals by Michel Goulet, Tim Kerr and Wayne Gretzky. As of 1998-99, Grant Fuhr has given up five 50th goals.

8.19 B. Three minutes

Robbie Irons's brief tenure as an NHL netminder lasted only three minutes but earned him everlasting fame as the goalie with the shortest career in the league. A career IHLer, Irons's quick-as-an-eye-blink shift occurred on November 13, 1968, in a game between New York and St. Louis. Glenn Hall and Jacques Plante were the Blues' tandem, but on that night Plante sat in the stands nursing a slight groin pull while Irons backed up Hall. Early in the game Hall received a game misconduct, forcing St. Louis coach Scotty Bowman to go with Irons. Scotty instructed the third stringer to take his warmup, then feign an equipment problem to delay the game until Plante was dressed. But Bowman's stalling tactics earned a penalty warning from referee Very Buffey. So out skated Irons, who played three minutes without facing a single shot on net. By 5:01 of the first period Plante was ready; Irons was yanked, never to play another second in the big leagues.

GAME 8

WAYNE GRETZKY'S FAVOURITE TARGETS

Wayne Gretzky embarrassed a lot of goalies on his way to becoming hockey's all-time leading scorer. Match the Gretzky milestone goal, assist or point and the netminder (or empty-net team) who/ that gave up the famous marker.

(Solutions are on page 121)

Empty net against Vancouver	Buffalo's Don Edwards
Edmonton's Bill Ranford	Vancouver's Glen Hanlon
Vancouver's Kirk McLean	Minnesota's Gary Edwards
Los Angeles' Mike Blake	Empty net against Philadelphia

1. _____ Wayne's first NHL goal (1979).

2. _____ Wayne's first 50th goal (1980).

3. _____ Wayne's 50th goal in 39 games (1981).

4. _____ Wayne's 77th goal of 1981-82, which broke Phil Esposito's single-season record (1982).

5. _____ Wayne's 92nd goal of 1981-82, the NHL's highest single-season total.

6. _____ Wayne's 500th goal, the NHL's fastest 500th (1986).

7. _____ Wayne's all-time point record: 1,851 points (1989).

8. _____ Wayne's 802nd goal, which broke Gordie Howe's record (1994).

9

MONEY MEN

Only one goalie won the Stanley Cup by overcoming a three-games-to-none deficit in the finals. The year was 1942, and gutsy fifth-place Detroit staged a remarkable semifinal series upset over first-place New York. More impressive, the Wings stormed Toronto in the finals with three consecutive wins, just one victory shy of the championship. Backstopped by Turk Broda, perhaps old-time hockey's best money goalie, the Maple Leafs regrouped and rebounded to win the Cup in the next four straight games. Broda notched a shutout in the come-back and in Game 7 stonewalled Detroit shooters in the 3-1 Cup winner. It was described as the wildest Stanley Cup series on record. In our final chapter we take the play to another level and look at some of the Stanley Cup's best money men.

(Answers are on page 110)

9.1 If the NHL mark for most Stanley Cups won by a skater is 11 championships, what is the Cup record for a goalie?
A. Five Stanley Cups
B. Six Stanley Cups
C. Seven Stanley Cups
D. Eight Stanley Cups

9.2 Which goalie faced the most shots in a Stanley Cup playoff year (since 1983-84 when shots on goal were first tabulated)?
A. Philadelphia's Ron Hextall in 1987
B. Los Angeles' Kelly Hrudey in 1993
C. Vancouver's Kirk McLean in 1994
D. Washington's Olaf Kolzig in 1998

9.3 Which goalie recorded the most overtime wins in one playoff season?
A. Billy Smith of the Islanders in 1980
B. Grant Fuhr of Edmonton in 1985
C. Patrick Roy of Montreal in 1993
D. Kirk McLean of Vancouver in 1994

9.4 How many starting goalies won Stanley Cups in the 1970s?
A. Three starting goalies
B. Four starting goalies
C. Five starting goalies
D. Six starting goalies

9.5 Who is the only goalie of the 1990s to record a shutout in his first career playoff game?
A. Calgary's Trevor Kidd
B. Toronto's Felix Potvin
C. Detroit's Chris Osgood
D. Pittsburgh's Frank Pietrangelo

9.6 Who is the only goalie to captain a Stanley Cup champion?
A. Montreal's Bill Durnan
B. Toronto's Turk Broda
C. Detroit's Johnny Mowers
D. Chicago's Chuck Gardiner

9.7 Which goalie of the 1990s won the longest 1-0 game in the history of the Stanley Cup finals?
A. Florida's John Vanbiesbrouck
B. Detroit's Mike Vernon
C. New Jersey's Martin Brodeur
D. Colorado's Patrick Roy

9.8 Which two modern-day goalies established the highest goal count (15 goals) for both teams in a Stanley Cup finals game?
A. The Islanders' Billy Smith and Edmonton's Grant Fuhr
B. Montreal's Ken Dryden and Chicago's Tony Esposito
C. Minnesota's Jon Casey and Pittsburgh's Tom Barrasso
D. Detroit's Mike Vernon and Philadelphia's Ron Hextall

9.9 Which Stanley Cup-winning goalie had the best goals-against average in playoff action during the 1990s?
A. New York's Mike Richter in 1994
B. New Jersey's Martin Brodeur in 1995
C. Colorado's Patrick Roy in 1996
D. Detroit's Mike Vernon in 1997

9.10 How many times in NHL history have rookies started in nets for an entire Stanley Cup final series?
A. It's never happened
B. Only once
C. Two times
D. Five times

9.11 Who was the oldest goalie to win the Stanley Cup?
A. Johnny Bower
B. Glenn Hall
C. Patrick Roy
D. Mike Vernon

9.12 Which goalie played the most minutes in a playoff year without winning the Stanley Cup?
A. Philadelphia's Ron Hextall in 1987
B. Montreal's Patrick Roy in 1989
C. Minnesota's Jon Casey in 1991
D. Vancouver's Kirk McLean in 1994

9.13 What is the fastest time in which a netminder gave up a goal in overtime in the playoffs? Name the goalie.
A. Nine seconds
B. 19 seconds
C. 29 seconds
D. 39 seconds

9.14 As of 1997-98, which goalie played in the most playoff games without winning the Stanley Cup?
A. Ed Belfour
B. Tony Esposito
C. Kelly Hrudey
D. Ron Hextall

9.15 What is the greatest number of different teams a goalie has played with and won the Stanley Cup?
A. Two different teams
B. Three different teams
C. Four different teams
D. Five different teams

9.16 What is the fewest goals allowed by a goalie in a best-of-seven Stanley Cup final series?
A. No goals
B. Two goals
C. Four goals
D. Six goals

9.17 Which goalie did Phil Esposito call "a thieving giraffe" in the 1970s?
A. Philadelphia's Bernie Parent
B. Montreal's Ken Dryden
C. The Soviet Union's Vladislav Tretiak
C. Chicago's Tony Esposito

9.18 Among the four NHLers who won the Conn Smythe Trophy as playoff MVP but lost the Stanley Cup, how many were goalies?
A. No goalie ever earned playoff MVP status and lost the Cup
B. Only one goalie earned playoff MVP status and lost the Cup
C. Two goalies earned playoff MVP status and lost the Cup
D. Three goalies earned playoff MVP status and lost the Cup

9.19 Which Stanley Cup-winning goalie since 1967 has had the biggest difference in his goals-against average between the regular season and the playoffs in which he won the Cup?
A. Patrick Roy
B. Gerry Cheevers
C. Rogatien Vachon
D. Tom Barrasso

MONEY MEN
Answers

9.1 B. Six Stanley Cups
Toronto's Turk Broda won a record five Stanley Cups during the Maple Leafs' dynasty years of the 1940s, but was eclipsed in the next decade by Jacques Plante, who won six championships with Montreal. That record was later tied by fellow Canadiens netminder and six-time Cup winner Ken Dryden, during the 1970s. Interestingly, Broda probably would have captured a sixth Cup with Toronto in 1944-45 had he not served in World War II. But it was Plante who had the best chance of increasing his Cup count. Had Montreal not traded him for Gump Worsley in 1963, Plante could have played out the decade with the dynasty Canadiens and won another four Cups. (This is a reasonable assumption, considering Plante was no older than Worsley and was still at the top of his game in 1969, the year he won his sixth Vezina Trophy—with Glenn Hall of St. Louis—and the same year Montreal—with Gump Worsley—won its fourth Stanley Cup of the 1960s.)

9.2   C. Vancouver's Kirk McLean in 1994

In 1994, McLean became the busiest goalie in postseason action when he faced a record 820 shots while appearing in 24 playoff games—a 31.9 shots-per-game average. Despite his workload, McLean still lost the championship. He bowed out in a Game 7 3-2 heartbreaker to the New York Rangers and goalie Mike Richter, who handled 623 shots over 23 games for a 26.4 average. Interestingly, four out of the five highest shots-against marks belong to Stanley Cup-losing goalies.

The NHL's Top 10 Most-Worked Playoff Goalies*

Player	Team	Season	GP/Mins	SA	SAPG
Kirk McLean	Van	1993-94	24/1544	820	31.9
Ron Hextall	Phi	1986-87	26/1540	769	30.0
Olaf Kolzig	Was	1997-98	21/1351	740	32.9
Bill Ranford	Edm	1989-90	22/1401	672	28.8
Kelly Hrudey	L.A.	1992-93	20/1261	656	31.2
Patrick Roy	Col	1995-96	22/1454	649	26.8
Patrick Roy	Mtl	1992-93	20/1293	647	30.0
Felix Potvin	Tor	1992-93	21/1308	636	29.2
Tom Barrasso	Pit	1990-91	20/1175	629	32.1
Mike Richter	NYR	1993-94	23/1417	623	26.4

From 1983-84 to 1997-98

9.3   C. Patrick Roy of Montreal in 1993

Roy's prominence among his peers has been built on a number of defining moments. The Canadiens' unlikely run at the Stanley Cup in 1993 was one of Roy's finest hours. Backstopping an almost-ordinary Habs team through 20 playoff games, Roy shut the door in 10 straight overtimes, giving Montreal skaters time to score the game winner in sudden-death play. No team had ever won more than six overtimes in one playoff year. Player for player, the Canadiens were in "the zone" behind Roy, literally chuckling to each other in the dressing room before overtime, trying to guess who would score the next overtime winner.

9.4 A. Three starting goalies
Three teams split a decade of Stanley Cups in the 1970s: Montreal won six in front of Ken Dryden; Boston and Philadelphia split the other four with Gerry Cheevers and Bernie Parent.

9.5 C. Detroit's Chris Osgood
A number of rookie goalies have bagged shutouts in their first playoff game, but Osgood is the only one to do it in the 1990s. On April 20, 1994, Osgood, in his first postseason game, stoned San Jose 4-0 in Game 2 of the Red Wings' seven-game series loss to the Sharks. The first rookie to collect a playoff zero in his first game is New York's Lorne Chabot, who recorded a scoreless tie with Hal Winkler of Boston in April 1927.

9.6 D. Chicago's Chuck Gardiner
Only a handful of goalies have served as team captains; just one, the great Chuck Gardiner, captained his team to a Stanley Cup title. Gardiner was handed the captaincy in 1933-34 after six seasons with the Blackhawks, a perennial cellar dweller that once set the record for fewest goals scored. Despite the lack of support, Gardiner maintained consistently solid averages, won two Vezina Trophies (top goalie) and was named to four All-Star teams. During 1933-34, Gardiner was instrumental in the Hawks' second-place finish, even though the club had the league's worst offensive record. It was no secret that throughout that regular-season campaign, Gardiner suffered from headaches so severe that at times he clutched the goalposts to keep from collapsing. Still, Gardiner limited the first-place Red Wings to two goals in his club's three victories. In the Stanley Cup clincher, Gardiner made 40 saves, shutting out the Wings 1-0 in a rare double overtime victory. It was the Blackhawks' first Stanley Cup. Two months later, Gardiner, only 29 years old, died of a brain hemorrhage. The Hawks honoured their fallen chief by not appointing a player to the captaincy the following season, one of the few occasions in Chicago's 70-year history that the club played without a captain.

9.7 D. Colorado's Patrick Roy
On June 10, 1996, Patrick Roy and John Vanbiesbrouck met in Game 4 of the Stanley Cup finals. Both were absolutely brilliant, but Roy stopped all 63 shots before teammate Uwe Krupp scored the Cup winner after five gruelling periods of play at 4:31 of triple overtime. The victory, the longest 1-0 game in finals history, capped an Avalanche four-game sweep over the Florida Panthers.

9.8 B. Montreal's Ken Dryden and Chicago's Tony Esposito
The 1973 Stanley Cup set a number of individual and team marks in finals action, including a record 56 goals by both Chicago and Montreal in the six-game round. It was a shooter's match as Dryden and Esposito performed like sieves in four double-digit scoring games. By far, the worst night, Game 5 on May 8, 1973, saw the Blackhawks score eight times on Dryden as Esposito, no less embarrassing, walked away with a win after giving up seven Canadiens goals. The 15-goal count broke a 37-year record, established in 1936 when Detroit and Toronto exploded for 13 goals in the Red Wings' 9-4 win. In the 1973 series, the lowest scores were Dryden's 4-0 and 4-1 wins. The other four contests were double-digit affairs of 10- , 11- , 11- and 15-goal games. Dryden allowed 23 goals and Esposito 33 as Montreal won the Cup. Eight months earlier Esposito and Dryden had been former teammates for Canada in the 1972 Summit Series against the Soviet Union.

9.9 B. New Jersey's Martin Brodeur in 1995
Brodeur sparkled with a rock-bottom 1.67 goals-against average on 34 goals during the Devils' 20-game romp to the Stanley Cup in 1995. Mike Vernon posted the next-best average (1.76) during the 1990s in Detroit's Cup win in 1997.

9.10 C. Two times
Every time rookies have faced each other in the Stanley Cup finals, something special has happened. The first rookies to meet in the finals were Toronto's Frank McCool and Detroit's Harry Lumley, in 1945. Far from the expected shooter's free-for-all,

McCool posted shutouts in the first three games to set a Stanley Cup record. Then Lumley responded with two of his own in Games 5 and 6 to tie the series. McCool won the Cup with a 2-1 victory in Game 7 but never played in another final series. In his 16-year career, Lumley went to the finals three more times, finally winning a Cup in 1949-50 in another seven-game series with Detroit. The next time another rookie-versus-rookie matchup occurred was 41 years later, when Mike Vernon and Patrick Roy manned opposing nets in the 1986 Montreal-Calgary Stanley Cup playoffs. The Canadiens easily handled the Flames and 22-year-old Roy became the youngest playoff MVP ever. Only one other freshman duel took place in finals action, but it involved Maple Leaf veteran netminder Turk Broda, who played the first two games of the classic 1951 Toronto-Montreal showdown between rookies Al Rollins of Toronto and Gerry McNeil of Montreal. After Broda, the veteran, split overtimes with McNeil in Games 1 and 2, Rollins, the rookie, returned from a knee injury to win the next three from the Canadiens, all in extra periods. It marked the first and only time in Stanley Cup history that every game of a final series ended in overtime. Another oddity in playoff rookie matchups.

9.11 A. Johnny Bower

When playoff MVP Mike Vernon led Detroit to the 1997 Stanley Cup, the veteran netminder was 34 years old. Although he was considered in the twilight of his career, Vernon was still eight years younger than Bower, who won the 1967 Cup with Toronto at age 42. Remarkably, like many old-timers with lengthy careers, Bower didn't hang up the pads when he won the Cup. He played two more seasons, quitting in 1969 after playing his last postseason. He was 44. (Although Lester Patrick, coach of the 1928 Cup-winning New York Rangers, was 45 years old when he stepped between the pipes for a half-game, he was not an active player.)

9.12 D. Vancouver's Kirk McLean in 1994

Vancouver's path to the 1994 Stanley Cup finals rested on the shoulder pads of Kirk McLean, who faced six overtimes and won five to advance to the final round. In Game 1 of the finals against New York, McLean won another overtime before the Rangers took the next three games straight. Up against the wall, the Canucks rallied with two victories, setting the stage for a Game 7 winner-take-all bout. Viewed by a record television audience worldwide, New York eked out a 3-2 win for the Cup, leaving McLean and the Canucks heartbroken after coming so far only to lose by one goal. McLean's Cup-less march totalled 1,554 minutes (about 26 games of postseason action), a new record that bested Ron Hextall's 1987 mark of 1,540 minutes by just four minutes. Among the top five goalies in this category, only leaders McLean and Hextall have never won the Stanley Cup.

9.13 A. Nine seconds

On May 18, 1986, Calgary's Mike Vernon was beaten just nine seconds into overtime on a goal by Brian Skrudland in a 3-2 Canadiens victory. The goal, scored in Game 2 of the Stanley Cup finals, set a new record for the fastest overtime goal (and shortest overtime period) in playoff history, passing the old mark of 11 seconds established by Jean-Paul Parise of the New York Islanders in 1975.

9.14 D. Ron Hextall

As of 1997-98, Hextall has worked more playoff games without winning the Stanley Cup than any other netminder in history. In fact, Hextall, Cup-less after 93 playoff matches, also leads all goalies with a frustration quotient of 10 final games in two final series losses (1987 and 1997). Other netminders have lost two championships in the finals, including Boston's Reggie Lemelin (1988 and 1990); Hank Bassen of Detroit (1961 and 1966); and the Wings' Roger Crozier, who had eight final game appearances (in 1966 and 1975). Tony Esposito, our trick choice, also lost twice in the finals (1971 and 1973) and backstopped Chicago for 99 playoff games without ever winning the Cup, but in his rookie season he was a third stringer with Montreal's Cup champions of 1969.

9.15 B. Three different teams

Although a few modern goalies, such as Patrick Roy, have succeeded in leading two different teams to the Stanley Cup, no one can match Harry "Hap" Holmes's four championships with three NHL clubs. During his 17-year career, the journeyman goalie played in four pro leagues, winning four Cups with the 1914 Toronto Blueshirts, the 1917 Seattle Metropolitans, the 1918 Toronto Arenas and the 1925 Victoria Cougars. Holmes's versatility and "nerveless" cage work earned him Hall of Fame status and his name on the American Hockey League's top goalie award, the Hap Holmes Memorial Trophy.

9.16 B. Two goals

The 1952 Stanley Cup finals may be old-time hockey's most convincing series of wins by an NHL champion. Detroit sophomore Terry Sawchuk established his playoff credentials, sweeping Toronto 4-0 in games in the first series, then, in the finals, recorded two shutouts and held Montreal to just two goals in another four-game sweep. Tied with Sawchuk is Ottawa's Alex Connell, who allowed just two goals in 1927's best-of-five series against Boston. In 1952, the Red Wings set an NHL benchmark by winning all eight postseason matches; Sawchuk, on five goals in eight playoff games, recorded a stingy 0.63, the lowest single-season average in modern-day playoff history.

9.17 B. Montreal's Ken Dryden

No one player was more responsible for stealing the Stanley Cup from the heavily favoured Boston Bruins in 1971 than the Canadiens' Ken Dryden. Not yet a rookie (just six NHL games to his credit), Dryden came out of nowhere and burned Phil Esposito, Bobby Orr and the first-place Bruins in the quarterfinals, staging one of the greatest heists in playoff history. Similar to today's Dominik Hasek, Dryden was a "sprawler" with a nimble, acrobatic style that defied the awkwardness of his six-foot-four frame. He lunged and smothered pucks; along the ice his stick and catching glove became extensions of his swooping torso and gangly arms and legs. A frustrated Esposito called Dryden "a thieving giraffe" during the 1971 upset.

9.18 D. Three goalies earned playoff MVP status and lost the Cup

Since 1965, when the Conn Smythe Trophy was awarded to the first playoff MVP, only four members from losing teams have earned the award. Among the quartet, three MVPs are goalies who, despite losing the championship, took home the Conn Smythe for their extraordinary play. The first MVP-winning goalie was Detroit's Roger Crozier, in 1966. Outpowered by heavily favoured Montreal, Crozier kept the long-shot Red Wings alive to survive six games, including surprising early back-to-back wins at the Montreal Forum. During Game 4, Crozier went down with a wrenched leg and the Wings lost confidence. He returned with a heavily taped knee only to lose Game 5 5-1 and Game 6 3-2, an overtime heartwrencher. The other two Cup-losing MVP goalies are St. Louis' Glenn Hall (in 1968) and Ron Hextall of Philadelphia (in 1987).

9.19 C. Rogatien Vachon

A few goalies have cut their regular-season goals-against averages by as much as a goal during the playoffs, but Vachon dropped the greatest amount since expansion in 1967. Splitting Montreal's goaltending duties with Gump Worsley in 1968-69, Vachon lowered his 2.87 goals-against average in 36 regular-season games to 1.42 in eight playoffs games, a drop of almost one and half goals per game. In the finals Vachon limited St. Louis to three goals in four games and registered his first playoff shutout. Other significant goals-against differences: in 1992-93, Roy's average dipped from 3.20 to 2.13, and Barrasso's from 3.59 to 2.60 in 1990-91.

SOLUTIONS TO GAMES

Game 1: BEEZER AND THE EAGLE

1. Curtis Joseph — H. CuJo
2. Felix Potvin — I. The Cat
3. Mike Vernon — U. Vernie
4. John Vanbiesbrouck — S. Beezer
5. Ed Belfour — L. The Eagle
6. Tom Barrasso — C. Tomcat
7. Mike Richter — V. Ricky Rod
8. Ron Hextall — P. Hexy
9. Martin Brodeur — M. Brody, or the Door
10. Dominik Hasek — A. The Dominator
11. Andre Racicot — K. Red Light
12. Grant Fuhr — J. Coco
13. Jim Carey — F. The Mask
14. Andy Moog — O. Mooger
15. Bill Ranford — W. Billy the Kid
16. Kirk McLean — N. Captain Kirk
17. Olie Kolzig — B. Godzilla, or Olie the Goalie
18. Jocelyn Thibault — Q. T-Bo
19. Trevor Kidd — G. Kidder
20. Arturs Urbe — T. Archie
21. Chris Osgood — E. The Wizard of Oz
22. Tommy Salo — R. Super Salo
23. Patrick Roy — D. St. Patrick

Game 2: ROOKIE WONDERS

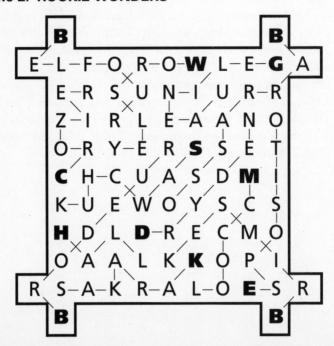

Game 3: "I STITCH BETTER WHEN MY SKIN IS SMOOTH"

1. Gilles Gratton. One of the game's flakiest goalies, Gratton believed in reincarnation. Seriously.

2. Lorne Chabot, on being asked why he always shaved before a game. Chabot played in the era before masks.

3. Dominik Hasek, the only netminder to face three straight 2,000-shot seasons (as of 1998-99).

4. Johnny Bower, on deciding to be a goaltender.

5. Glenn Hall, who also said, "Playing goal is a winter of torture for me," puked before almost every game of his 1,021-game career. Hall raised his family in Stoney Plain, Alberta.

6. Terry Sawchuk, who probably suffered more injuries than any other goalie in NHL history.

7. John Vanbiesbrouck, questioned if he liked facing 51 shots in a game.

8. Gump Worsley, one of hockey's most quotable.

9. After nine shots, Glenn Resch hit the Islander goalposts during a playoff series against the Pittsburgh Penguins.

Game 4: THE HOCKEY CROSSWORD

Game 5: NET WORTH

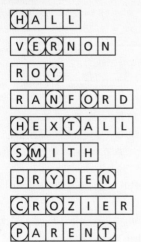

HALL
VERNON
ROY
RANFORD
HEXTALL
SMITH
DRYDEN
CROZIER
PARENT

CONN SMYTHE TROPHY

Donated by Maple Leaf Gardens Limited to honour former coach, manager and president Conn Smythe, the Conn Smythe Trophy is awarded annually to the playoffs' most valuable player. Between 1964 and 1998 nine goalies have won the trophy 11 times.

Game 6: PICK OF THE PACK

1.	G.	Tom Barrasso 5th overall by Buffalo
2.	I.	Grant Fuhr 8th overall by Edmonton
3.	F.	Martin Brodeur 20th overall by New Jersey
4.	K.	Sean Burke 24th overall by New Jersey
5.	M.	Mike Richter 28th overall by the Rangers
6.	E.	Felix Potvin 31st overall by Toronto
7.	O.	Patrick Roy 51st overall by Montreal
8.	A.	Bill Ranford 52nd overall by Boston
9.	B.	John Vanbiesbrouck 72nd overall by the Rangers
10.	L.	Kirk McLean 107th overall by Vancouver
11.	N.	Ron Hextall 119th overall by Philadelphia
12.	D.	Andy Moog 132nd overall by Edmonton
13.	J.	Dominik Hasek 199th overall by Chicago
14.	C.	Ed Belfour signed as a free agent by Chicago in 1987
15.	H.	Curtis Joseph signed as a free agent by St. Louis in 1989

Game 7: LAST LINE OF DEFENSE

All 27 goalies are V-E-Z-I-N-A T-R-O-P-H-Y W-I-N-N-E-R-S.

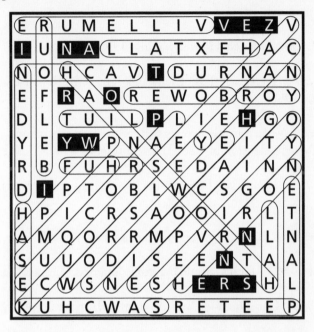

Game 8: WAYNE GRETZKY'S FAVOURITE TARGETS

1. In 1979 Vancouver's Glen Hanlon gave up Wayne's first NHL goal.

2. In 1980 Minnesota's Gary Edwards allowed Wayne's first 50th goal.

3. In 1981 an empty net goal against Philadelphia set the record for Wayne's 50th goal in 39 games.

4. In 1982 Buffalo's Don Edwards gave up Wayne's 77th goal of 1981-82, breaking Phil Esposito's single-season record.

5. Los Angeles' Mike Blake let in Wayne's 92nd goal of 1981-82, the NHL's highest single-season total.

6. In 1986 an empty net against Vancouver allowed Wayne's 500th goal, the NHL's fastest 500th.

7. In 1989 Edmonton's Bill Ranford was in nets for Wayne's all-time point-scoring record: 1,851 points.

8. In 1994 Vancouver's Kirk McLean gave up Wayne's 802nd goal, breaking Gordie Howe's record.

ACKNOWLEDGEMENTS

Thanks to the following publishers and organizations for the use of quoted material:

A Breed Apart. Douglas Hunter. Viking, 1995.

The Death of Hockey. Jeff Z. Klein and Karl-Eric Reif. Macmillan Canada, 1998.

The Hockey News, various excerpts. Reprinted by permission of the *Hockey News*, a division of GTC, Transcontinental Publishing, Inc.

In the Crease. Dick Irvin Enterprises. McClelland and Stewart, Inc., 1995.

Of Ice and Men. Bruce Dowbiggin. MacFarlane, Walter & Ross, 1998.

Sawchuk. David Dupuis. Stoddard Publishing Co., Limited, 1998.

Total Hockey. Dan Diamond and Associates, Inc. Total Sports, 1998.

Care has been taken to trace ownership of copyright material contained in this book. The publishers welcome any information that will enable them to rectify in subsequent editions any reference or credit that is inaccurate.

The author gratefully acknowledges the help of Gary Meagher and Benny Ercolani of the NHL; Phil Prichard, Craig Campbell and Jeff Davis at the Hockey Hall of Fame; the sports broadcasters at CFCF 12 in Montreal; the staff at the McLellan-Redpath Library at McGill University; Rob Sanders, Terry Wershler and Leanne Denis at Greystone Books; the many hockey writers and broadcasters who have made the game better through their own work; my Webmaster Mike Curran; Kerry Banks, who made so many saves so many times with his fact checking and editing; and editor Anne Rose, graphic artist Peter van Vlaardingen and puzzle designer Adrian van Vlaardingen for their outstanding work.